Summits
of the
South

Visitor's Guide to 25
Southern Appalachian Mountains

compiled by Brian Boyd

Fern Creek Press

i

Summits of the South
ISBN # 0-9625737-5-2
Published by Fern Creek Press
PO Box 1322
Clayton, GA 30525

Copyright © 1992 Fern Creek Press

• Special thanks to Beaver Koch and my dad, Larry Boyd, for putting up with me on these summit hikes. A very special "thank you" to Gap Graphics and Printing, Mountain City, GA, for allowing the use of their computer equipment in typesetting this book.

The author and publisher of this guidebook assume no responsibility for any loss of property, accident, injury or death sustained while visiting any of the locations described in this guidebook. The very nature of the mountains in this guidebook make them potentially dangerous to visit. Please use caution and common sense when in the wild.

Cover: Sunset from Black Rock Mountain's Tennessee Rock Overlook. Insets: Snow atop Clingman's Dome. Autumn scene looking toward Whiteside Mountain.

Summits of the South

Contents

Climb the mountains,
   and get their good tidings...
      Nature's peace will flow into you
         as sunshine flows into trees...

The winds will blow
   their freshness into you,
      and the storms their energy...
         While cares will drop off
            like autumn leaves.

- John Muir

INTRODUCTION

Just what is it about a mountain that attracts humans so strongly? How does one describe that near-mystical pull that they exert on us? For some, it may be the challenge of the climb, the hike, the conquering of the peak. For others, it is the view - unrestricted, unencumbered, inspiring. Still others seek the solitude, the aloneness that can only be attained, perhaps captured, atop some majestic peak.

Regardless of what attracts us, the fact remains that these high places - mountains, peaks, summits - are some of the most popular destinations to be explored anywhere. Here in the South, the ancient Southern Appalachians are more than a mere mountain chain, they define a way of life. Visitors come from across the country to explore the region, and sooner or later find their way to one of these timeless peaks. The Smokies, the Blue Ridge, the Black Mountains, The Cowees, the Nantahalas - they are all unique and remarkably different areas of the same grand region.

The overall purpose of **Summits of the South** is to offer the casual visitor a wide range of options to consider when visiting these impressive peaks. This guidebook contains 25 different summits, scattered across North Georgia, western North Carolina, eastern Tennessee and western South Carolina. Several of these peaks can be easily visited via auto, with little walking required to reach the top. Others feature short, easy trails to the summit, while still more require varying hikes ranging from 0.25 mile to 10 miles and more. Whatever your skill level, whatever your taste, these scenic wonders await you - each with its own interesting history, geology, and personality. These peaks range from relatively obscure to grand and famous, from long ridgelines to narrow, funnelling peaks, but they all have one thing in common - each has its own inspiring view to reward those who choose to visit them. Grab your hiking shoes and camera, pack a lunch, and come explore these southern treasures, these **Summits of the South**.

Summits

of the

South

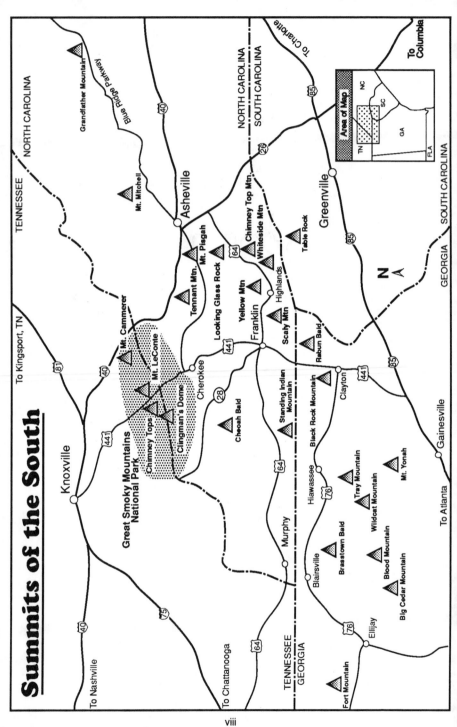

Summits of the South

North Georgia Summits

Yonah Mountain (3,156')

• **Chattahoochee National Forest, GA**

• **Length: approx. 1.0 mile round trip**
• **Difficulty: moderate**
• **Overall elevation gain: approx. 400 feet**

Yonah Mountain is a landmark peak to those who have visited the Cleveland, GA. area. Yonah, Cherokee for "Bear", rises over 1,000 feet above the rolling hillsides of scenic White County, its rocky upper cliffs distinguishing it from other area summits. Long popular among advanced rock climbers and repellers, this peak offers something more to the summit-lover-mainly unrestricted views of the Southern Blue Ridge chain of Northeast Georgia. Perhaps dismissed by some as being insignificant, I have personally found the views from Yonah to be a real sleeper among southern peaks - a sleeper waiting to be explored.

To reach Yonah's wooded crown, you and your vehicle must negotiate 2.5 miles of washboard quality dirt road to the flat, open parking area nestled among giant, shady hardwoods. It is here that you will first encounter Yonah's major drawback - trash. Evidence of campers and weekend visitors is everywhere. As you will unfortunately discover, this problem is widespread all across the mountainface. Do everyone a favor and bring a trashbag!

The Trail: From the parking area, numerous routes to the summit are possible. A gated service road winds to the top, still some 0.5 miles distant. Any number of obscure paths snake upward across the narrowing peak. The climb to the summit from the parking area is approximately 400 feet, quite deceiving to first-timers. The stairstepping nature of the mountain prevents a clear view of the top from the parking area.

Perhaps the best route is to follow the trails that slant to the right when you are in sight of the rocky southern face. This is perhaps only 5 minutes from the parking area. Several of these trails wind through a boulder field and traverse the edges of dangerous, sheer cliffs. Marvelous views of the undulating hills and ridges below are clearly visible. Continue upward and you will attain the top of the cliffs, where repellers come from across the region to challenge Yonah's dangerous but enticing rock face. From this open rocky area, panoramic views of some of Georgia's most famous summits are visible - Brasstown Bald, Blood Moun-

2

tain, Tray Mountain - a veritable who's who among Georgia peaks. Atlanta's ever-growing skyline can be clearly seen on ultra-clear days, almost due south. The town of Cleveland, as well as farms, towns, lakes and fields, unfold below you and compete for your attention.

Just above this rocky grandstand, the summit features a large grassy field surrounded by hardwoods. Like many other southern summits, trees at the actual highpoint block the best views. The area is popular as a camping spot, though, as numerous fire rings attest. The easiest descent is along the service road, which heads down from the eastern edge of the clearing.

Special Note: The US Army periodically trains its personnel in repelling on these cliffs. It would be a good idea to call ahead and inquire about military scheduling. Call (404) 864-3367 to find out about potential conflicts.

Directions: From Cleveland, head north along Hwy 75 toward Helen. Proceed 3.7 miles from the traffic light (at the Hwy 129/75 intersection) to the dirt road (#78) on the right, just next to the Yonah Mountain Campground. Proceed 2.5 miles along the lousy dirt road to the parking area. Note: A short side trail snakes down to the right just 0.1 mile before the parking area. This trail leads to the base of the cliffs, NOT to the summit.

Yonah Mountain

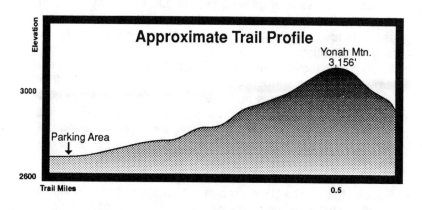

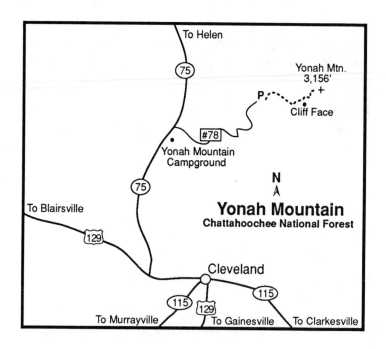

Fort Mountain (2,854')
- via Old Fort Trail
- Fort Mountain State Park

- Length: approx. 1.8 miles
- Difficulty: easy
- Overall elevation gain: approx. 200 feet

Perhaps lesser known and certainly less dramatic than many other Southern summits described in this book, Fort Mountain, at 2,854 feet, is nonetheless a worthy destination. Perched almost precariously along the eastern edge of the Great Valley region of north central Georgia, historic Fort Mountain is one of the western sentinels of the rugged Cohutta range.

The mountain features 1,932 acre Fort Mountain State Park, created after the 1929 donation of this property to the government by Ivan Allen, Sr. The scenery is spectacular, though perhaps not the main drawing card. Fort Mountain's prime attraction and namesake is an ancient, loosely stacked stone wall which measures 850 feet in length. This puzzling structure, long a source of speculation to archeologists and regional historians, ranges from about 2 to 6 feet high, and stretches east to west just below the peak's heavily wooded southern crown.

The Trail: Fort Mountain's summit is reached via the Old Fort Trail, a system of interlinking paths blazed in several colors. The trail originates in a parking area just past the Gahuti Trail starting point, near the Cool Springs Overlook. Officially, the Old Fort Trail is listed at 1.8 miles, though numerous paths crossing the area and meandering along the wall could bring the total up somewhat. The trail is a loop, and hikers may choose whichever direction they wish. The pathway climbs several hundred feet to the summit, and features Virginia Pine and mixed hardwoods, especially oaks. The views from the summit will be substantially better in the colder months, as heavy foliage and underbrush can obscure the view.

The trail snaking up Fort Mountain's western flank passes through a fragmented boulder field, shaded beneath gnarled, twisted oaks. Views of Chatsworth far below can be glimpsed through the forest canopy. Just minutes up the trail, the western end of the mysterious wall is encountered. A trail crosses east from here across the loop, along the wall's edge, and allows easy exploration of the wall. Continuing up the western flank, one soon comes to a side trail which winds out to the Chatsworth Overlook. This view westward includes breathtaking views of scenic ridges beyond the valley below. Towards the center of the loop trail, an old stone observation tower rises from the mountain's high point. This tower, nearly 40 feet tall, offers exciting panoramic views. Recently, however, the surrounding treeline has grown to the point where views will be restricted in the warmer months. Regardless of the season, however, Fort Mountain and its historic and mysterious past holds something for each visitor. And the view ain't bad, either.

Directions: From Chatsworth, take highway 52 east for 7 miles. Once inside the park, follow the main park road straight ahead to the dead-end parking area and trail head. Additional maps can be obtained at the park headquarters.

Alternate Hikes: Several other trails within the park offer varying challenges to hikers. These trails include the Gahuti Trail (8.2 mile loop trail), Big Rock Nature Trail (0.7 mile), and the Lake Loop Trail (1.1 miles).

Fort Mountain

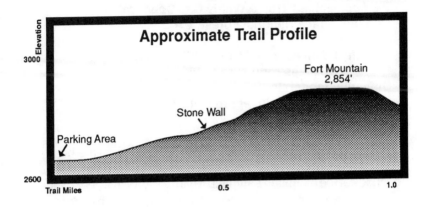

Approximate Trail Profile

Elevation

3000

Fort Mountain
2,854'

Stone Wall

Parking Area

2600

Trail Miles

0.5

1.0

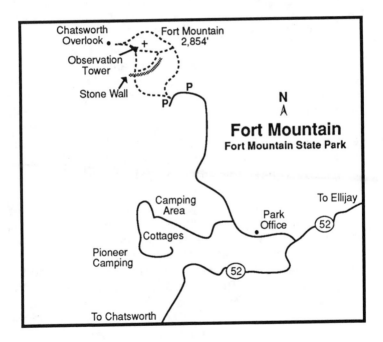

Chatsworth
Overlook

Fort Mountain
2,854'

Observation
Tower

Stone Wall

P

P

N

Fort Mountain
Fort Mountain State Park

Camping
Area

To Ellijay

Park
Office

52

Cottages

Pioneer
Camping

52

To Chatsworth

Wildcat Mountain (3,730')

- via Appalachian Trail & Whitly Gap Spur Trail
- Chattahoochee National Forest, GA

- Length: 1.5 miles round trip to Wildcat Mtn. summit
          2.6 miles round trip to Whitly Gap
- Difficulty: moderate
- Overall elevation gain: approx. 300 feet

A convenient and easily hiked trail snakes up the beautifully scenic ridgeline of Wildcat Mountain to an open, rocky overlook at the mountain's summit. This trail, the Whitly Gap Spur Trail, originates along the Appalachian Trail about 0.25 mile west of Hogpen Gap along Highway 348 (Richard Russell Scenic Highway). This popular spur trail goes up and over Wildcat Mountain, then descends into Whitly Gap to a trail shelter (and water source) 0.6 mile beyond the summit. This hike makes an ideal family trip, and is perfect for picnicing.

The Trail: From the Hogpen Gap parking area along the Union/White County line, Wildcat Mountain lies almost due south. To reach the Whitly Gap Spur Trail, begin along the Appalachian Trail segment that heads west from the gap. You will immediately enter the Raven Cliffs Wilderness Area and begin a steep switchbacking climb for 0.25 mile up to the ridgeline and the intersection with the Whitly Gap Spur Trail. At this junction, a sign denotes directions and distances - 1.1 miles south to Whitly Gap, and 0.9 mile west to Tesnatee Gap.

You may now breath a sigh of relief if Wildcat's rocky summit is your destination, as most of your strenuous climbing is now behind you. What lies ahead is a tremendously beautiful 0.5 mile stroll along a scenic, narrow ridgeline. The path is an absolute pleasure to traverse. The climb is minimal, and the scenery spectacular. The trail is often rocky, but mosses and lichens have covered most of the rocks and wild grasses grow neatly alongside. Thick tunnels of rhododendron smother the trail. Wildflowers abound, and ancient oaks grow gnarled and twisted along the ridgeline.

The elongated rocky ridge features stunning views to the south and west. Look for the summits of Hogpen Mountain to the west, and Blood Mountain's massive crown looms slightly north of west. Views in the other directions can be glimpsed, but one must explore among the side trails for openings in the thick forest canopy to find them. The summit is a very popular camping spot for backpackers, and visitors here should always help pack out the ever-present trash left behind. Wildcat's summit is surely a spot to linger, and it is a wonder that anyone continues the additional 0.6 mile to the Whitly Gap Shelter (unless they are going for the water).

The trail continues beyond the shelter, but soon begins to become less defined. Just beyond the shelter, numerous primitive camping sites lie beneath shady hardwoods, nestled among wild grasses. If you wish to camp and the summit of Wildcat is crowded, consider one of these peaceful sites.

Directions: From Helen, proceed north along Hwy 75 to the junction with Hwy 356. Turn left onto Hwy 356 and proceed 2.3 miles to Hwy 348 . Turn right onto Hwy 348 (Russell Scenic Highway) and proceed 7 miles to Hogpen Gap at the White / Union County line. The Appalachian Trail segment leading to the Whitly Gap Spur Trail begins on the opposite (south) side of the road from the parking area.

Wildcat Mountain

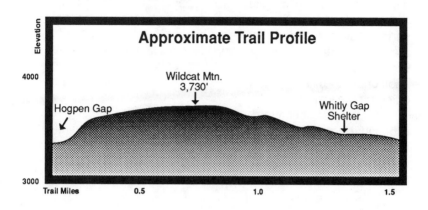

Approximate Trail Profile

Wildcat Mountain
via Appalachian Trail
& Whitly Gap Spur Trail

Big Cedar Mountain (3,737')

- via Appalachian Trail
- Chattahoochee National Forest, GA

- Length: 2 miles round trip
- Difficulty: easy to moderate
- Overall elevation gain: 600 feet

A relatively little-known, yet extremely beautiful summit, Big Cedar Mountain, can be reached via the popular Appalachian Trail by hiking 1 mile north from Woody Gap near the scenic mountain village of Suches. This short hike follows the 11.5 mile AT segment that includes rugged Blood Mountain and terminates at Neel's Gap (see Blood Mountain section). Big Cedar Mountain, at 3,737 feet, does not rate among the tallest of Georgia's peaks, nor is its heavily forested summit unusually special. Yet, the combination of easy access and a spectacular rocky outcrop near the summit give visitor's ample reason to visit this scenic peak. If the nearly 5 mile round trip and 1200 foot climb up Blood Mountain intimidates you, consider this easy 2 mile round trip walk and its much milder 600 foot ascent.

The Trail: This segment of the famous Appalachian Trail originates in the large gravel parking area at Woody Gap (3,160 feet). From this large, open gap, the white-blazed trail meanders along the heavily wooded slopes of Steel Trap, climbing easily before dropping into Lunsford Gap (3,330 feet) at mile 0.7. The pathway passes several scenic primitive camping sites nestled among large mature, hardwoods.

Just past the gap, the trail begins a moderately steep switchbacking climb up the southeastern slope of Big Cedar Mountain. The crooked path discects a rugged area of fragmented boulders, and several good vistas to the east can be glimpsed through the forest canopy. A large, open sloping rock outcrop is reached at mile 1.0 - known to many hiker's familiar with this portion of the AT as "Preacher's Rock." This smooth open grey slab appears just 0.3 mile shy of Big Cedar's summit, and is situated along a narrow ridgeline. As the path cuts steadily north, the sloping Preacher's Rock disappears abruptly off the mountain's east flank, and provides spectacular views, particularly of the Water's Creek watershed far below. The streams roar can be plainly heard from this outcrop, and contributes greatly to the wilderness atmosphere. Beyond, low peaks and ridges recede toward the Piedmont and horizon beyond. The distinctive profile of Mount Yonah near Cleveland dominates the view.

The actual summit, though only 0.3 mile beyond, is quite heaily wooded, and does not feature any open vistas. Consequently, you may wish to linger at Preacher's Rock and not bother with trying to gain a better view from the top. Backpackers and overnight campers may wish to set-up in one of the primitive camping spots at Preacher's Rock. Several campsites are located on the western side of the ridge, just yards off the main trail. From this western flank, cold season hikers can glimpse the picturesque farms and fields of Suches through bare limbs of the hardwood forest.

Directions: From Dahlonega, follow US 19 north to the US 19/ GA 60 split. Bear left and continue 5.4 miles to the Lumpkin/Union County line at Woody Gap. Park in the large gravel lot on the right side of the gap. The Appalachian Trail to Big Cedar Mountain heads right (north). There are picnic tables and toilet facilities at Woody Gap.

Alternate Hike: For those wishing to enjoy this segment to its fullest extent, the 11.5 mile section from Woody Gap to Neel's Gap makes an outstanding day hike or overnight trip. The hike features Blood Mountain's spectacular panoramas, and is a favorite of many veteran hikers.

Big Cedar Mountain

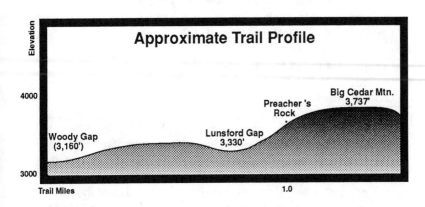

Approximate Trail Profile

Elevation

4000

Big Cedar Mtn.
3,737'

Preacher's
Rock

Woody Gap
(3,160')

Lunsford Gap
3,330'

3000

Trail Miles   1.0

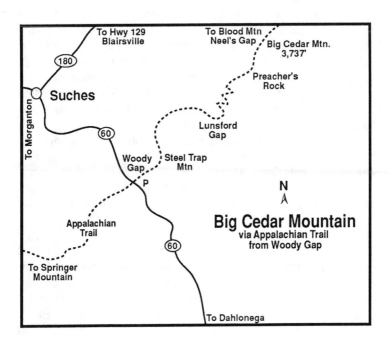

To Hwy 129
Blairsville

To Blood Mtn
Neel's Gap   Big Cedar Mtn.
3,737'

Preacher's
Rock

180

Suches

To Morganton

60

Lunsford
Gap

Woody
Gap

Steel Trap
Mtn

P

N

Big Cedar Mountain
via Appalachian Trail
from Woody Gap

Appalachian
Trail

60

To Springer
Mountain

To Dahlonega

Blood Mountain (4,458')

• via Appalachian Trail & Reece Spur Trail
• Chattahoochee National Forest, GA

• **Length: 4.4 miles round trip**
• **Difficulty: strenuous**
• **Overall elevation gain: 1,500 feet**

One of Georgia's most popular day hikes climbs 2.2 miles and nearly 1500 feet up rugged Blood Mountain. Named for a legendary Indian encounter hundreds of years ago, this wildly popular hike attracts throngs of visitors of all skill levels (and even some of no skill level). Sweeping panoramic vistas of the lush, surrounding valleys and bold peaks can be enjoyed from Blood's rocky summit.

Part of Blood Mountain's popularity is due to its convenient location along one of the most accessible portions of Georgia's Appalachian Trail segment. The pathway crosses Highway 19/129 in Neel's Gap, 18 miles north of Cleveland. Walasi-Yi interpretive center, a popular backpacking outfitter and gift shop, lies nestled in the gap, occupying an enchanting old stone and native wood building constructed in the mid 1930's by the Civilian Conservation Corps. A visit to Walasi-Yi is a must for any Blood Mountain hiker.

To avoid congestion in the cramped parking area at Walasi-Yi, a special Blood Mountain spur trail has been constructed 0.4 mile north of Neel's Gap. This blue-blazed connector trail originates in the Byron Herbert Reece Memorial Picnic Area, and provides the starting point for day hikes to the summit of Blood Mountain.

The trail: From the Reece Picnic Area (3000 foot elev.), the trail switchbacks moderately upward through varying stands of rhododendron and mixed hardwoods, snaking 0.7 mile to Flatrock Gap and the Appalachian Trail junction. One mile to the east of the junction is Neel's Gap, while 1.5 miles west (right) is the Blood Mountain summit. Just down the AT to the left is an interesting rock formation that gives Flatrock Gap its name. The area is also a perfect picnic spot.

Though many jokes have been made about how appropriate the name "Blood Mountain" is, the climb to the summit is not overly difficult. Generous switchbacks make the climb bearable, if somewhat unrelenting. The path alternates between sloping ridgeline and moderately steep switchbacks along its 1000 foot climb from Flatrock Gap, and traverses a fascinatingly wide range of vegetation. Mixed hardwoods give way to dense groves of rhododendron and native laurel. Wildflowers abound in the warmer months. Warm season hikers will enjoy the cool shade of the forest, while winter visitors are rewarded with stunning views through the bare hardwoods. Numerous boulders and rock slabs choke the trail in spots, and provide good places to catch one's breath along the ascent.

Shortly before attaining the summit, the path emerges onto a smooth, bare rock outcrop. Continue along the white painted trail markers toward the summit, now enticingly close. Chances are good that you will pass numerous tent campers through this section, as the rocky vantage point provides impressive views to the south and avoids the heavy hiker congestion at the summit, just moments ahead.

The 4,458 foot summit of Blood Mountain is draped with rhododendron, laurel, and gnarled hardwoods. Be sure to visit the old stone hiking shelter atop the mountain. This two room cabin, built in the 1930's, contains a native rock fireplace and sleeping platform for weather-weary hikers. It has been the sight of legendary partying over the years (if only the walls could talk!). Just behind the shelter several massive grey boulders provide the most popular spot on the summit to enjoy the panoramic view of this beautiful portion of North Georgia. Take along a Forest Service map and try your hand at identifying the many peaks, valleys and towns visible. Use caution and good sense here, especially if you are staying the night, as the boulders are very steep and treacherous. This summit is a spot to linger and savour. Best of all, it's all downhill from here!

Directions: From Cleveland, follow highway 129 north, or from Dahlonega, highway 19 north. The two highways merge and proceed north into Neel's Gap. The Appalachian Trail crosses the highway at Neel's Gap. The Walasi-Yi Center is to the right as you pass the gap. To reach the Reece trailhead, proceed 0.4 mile north. The picnic area and parking are to the left.

Alternate Hikes: There are several optional hikes from Neel's Gap. Those wishing a greater challenge may want to try the 11.7 mile one way hike from Woody Gap to Neel's Gap. This hike along the Appalachian Trail features the summits of Big Cedar and Blood Mountain, and can easily be walked in one day.

If the parking areas at Neel's Gap and the Reece Picnic Area are especially congested, you may want to avoid Blood Mountain completely. An easy, alternate walk to Levelland Mountain may be an option to consider. While the view from Levelland is not very dramatic, good vistas to the south can be gained from its nearly level ridgeline. The distance is 1.7 miles east along the Appalachian Trail. The gain in altitude is an easy 800 feet.

Blood Mountain

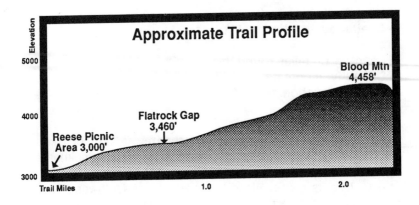

Approximate Trail Profile

Elevation

5000 — Blood Mtn 4,458'

4000 — Flatrock Gap 3,460'

Reese Picnic Area 3,000'

3000

Trail Miles   1.0   2.0

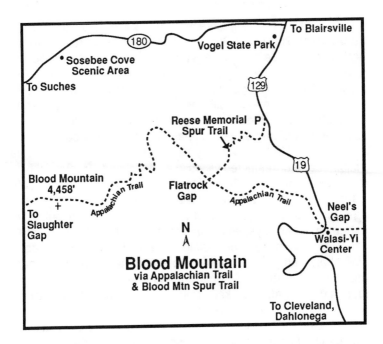

To Blairsville

180

Vogel State Park

• Sosebee Cove Scenic Area

To Suches

129

Reese Memorial   P Spur Trail

19

Blood Mountain 4,458'

Appalachian Trail

Flatrock Gap

Appalachian Trail

Neel's Gap

To Slaughter Gap

Walasi-Yi Center

N

Blood Mountain
via Appalachian Trail
& Blood Mtn Spur Trail

To Cleveland, Dahlonega

Tray Mountain (4,430')
- via Appalachian Trail
- Chattahoochee National Forest, GA

- Length: 1.8 miles round trip
- Difficulty: moderate
- Overall elevation gain: 600'

One of Georgia's most popular and rewarding short hikes climbs along the famous Appalachian Trail to the rocky topknot of Tray Mountain, located in the 9,700 acre Tray Mountain Wilderness. Like its cousin Blood Mountain to the southwest, Tray Mountain offers spectacular panoramic views of North Georgia. Unlike Blood, however, the hike to the top is relatively short and never exceeds a moderate degree of difficulty.

The Trail: From the intersection of FS 698, FS 79, and the Appalachian Trail (Tray Gap), it is only 0.9 mile to Tray's summit. Adding to the ease of this hike is the relatively mere 600 foot climb required. Broad, looping switchbacks easily traverse the rocky mountain face, gliding beneath red oaks and shady mixed hardwoods. Approximately 0.8 mile into the hike, a picturesque overlook is encountered to the left, offering a quick chance to catch one's breath before the final portion of the ascent.

Tray Mountain's rocky summit is quite small, but offers major league unrestricted views in all directions. Peaks such as Brasstown Bald and Blood Mountain are easily visible. Mt. Yonah's unmistakeable profile is prominent to the south. To the east, several narrow arms of Lake Burton stand out. On extremely clear days, landmarks to the south such as Atlanta's Stone Mountain become visible, as are peaks in the rugged Nantahala Range to the north. Purple rhododendron flourish near the top, and numerous gnarled and wind-stunted trees and shrubs crowd dense thickets around the summit. None of these pose a problem to the view, fortunately.

Several hundred yards north of Tray's highpoint, a short side trail branches from the Appalachian Trail, and runs off to the right out to an excellent southern overlook.

The Tray Mountain area becomes quite crowded on weekends and in the summer, so plan your trip accordingly. For those who can catch this mountain at the right time, though, Tray can be one of the South's most dramatic and easily reached summits. See you at the top!

Directions: There are numerous routes to Tray Gap, and none are particularly easy. The recommended route is to follow Hwy 75 north from Helen for 11 miles and turn right onto FS 283 (located 2 miles north of Unicoi Gap). At times, this gravel road is marked by a small sign announcing "High Shoals". You will know if you have the right road if you come to a stream which must be forded in your automobile just a few hundred yards from the highway. Proceed 4 miles along the bumpy road, then turn east onto FS 79. Proceed 2 miles along FS 79 to its junction with FS 698 and the Appalachian Trail. This is Tray Gap. There are several worn parking spaces on the opposite side of the road from the trail as it begins the ascent to the summit.

Additional Hiking: If you're still up to it after your climb, proceed back along FS 283 to the point 1.3 miles from the highway. Several parking spaces are located in a sharp turn, and the area is usually marked by a small sign. This is the trailhead for High Shoals Scenic Area - 170 acres of beautiful cascading streams and waterfalls. It is a steep 1.2 mile hike down to the last waterfall, but the walk is well worth the effort. Of particular interest are Blue Hole Falls and High Shoals Falls. This is a beautiful area and can be visited any time of the year.

Tray Mountain

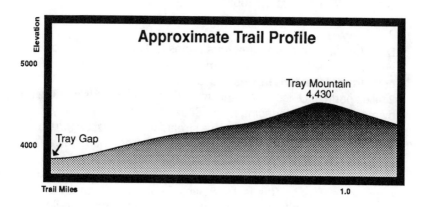

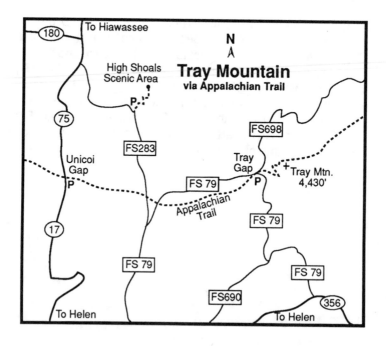

Brasstown Bald (4,784')

- via vehicle, various trails
- Chattahoochee National Forest, GA

- Length: 1.0 mile round trip or van shuttle to summit
- Difficulty: moderate
- Overall elevation gain: approx. 400 feet

Brasstown Bald Mountain is Georgia's highest summit, reaching 4,784 feet above sea level. Though it is certainly the state's most visited and developed peak, it is surrounded on 3 sides by the 11,405 acre Brasstown Wilderness Area. Visitors to this popular mountain can enjoy several interesting exhibits in a mountaintop visitors center, or just take in the view. What many visitors do not know, however, is that several challenging trails lace the summit, providing competent hikers with another reason to visit Brasstown Bald.

Casual visitors may reach the top of the mountain either by foot or by taking the shuttle van. A small charge gets you to the top fast, with an absolute minimal effort. Those brave souls who choose to attempt the 0.5 mile **paved** path to the top are rewarded with spectacular groves of gnarled rhododendron and laurel thickets, as well as good displays of wildflowers. It is surprising to see how many visitors (that look in otherwise good shape) actually wait to ride the van when the summit is so close!

The summit itself comprises nearly an acre, with the largest part being occupied by the large visitors complex. Things to see here include an excellent audio visual presentation on the mountain and its many features. There is also an exhibit detailing the history of the region and its inhabitants. Forest Service pesonnel are on hand to answer any questions you may have.

On the outside, a large circular observation deck is perched upon the roof of the building. Absolutely unencumbered views can be easily enjoyed from the platform. Portions of 4 states are easily visible on clear days, with points as far away as Atlanta visible. Particularly scenic views of Hiawassee and Lake Chatuge lie to the north.

As with other Southern Appalachian peaks of this magnitude, the weather can become interesting atop Brasstown Bald rather quickly. A warm, clear day in Helen or one of the other surrounding towns can fast become cold and windy on top of Brasstown Bald. Summertime temperatures rarely exceed the 80 degree mark, and are usually in the comfortable 70's. Be prepared for any type of weather at any time, especially if hiking the longer trails.

Brasstown Bald is normally open 10 a.m. to 5:30 p.m. daily from Memorial Day through October, and is usually open weekends in early spring and late fall, weather permitting. Call (706) 745-6928 for additional information.

Directions: Brasstown Bald is located off Hwy 180 approximately 6 miles west of Hwy 17/75. Hwy 180 Spur winds 3 miles up the mountain to the parking area. The trail to the top begins behind the concession shack.

Alternate Hikes: Three other long trails snake up the steep mountain, offering advanced hikers more of a challenge. The Jack's Knob Trail runs 4.5 miles down to Hwy 180 and a junction with the Appalachian Trail shortly beyond. The 5.5 mile Arkaquah Trail heads west down to the historic Track Rock Gap Archeological Area. The longest route is via the 7 mile Wagon Train Trail, following an old trail once intended to become GA 66. This trail emerges from the forest on the campus of Young Harris College in the town of Young Harris.

By the way, if you're wondering where "Brasstown" came from, it was evidently a misunderstanding of the Cherokee terms *itse-yi* which means "new green place" and *untsaiyi*, which means "brass". It seems there is never an interpreter around when you need one.

Brasstown Bald

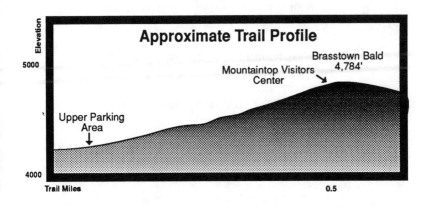

Approximate Trail Profile

Elevation

5000

Brasstown Bald
4,784'

Mountaintop Visitors
Center

Upper Parking
Area

4000

Trail Miles   0.5

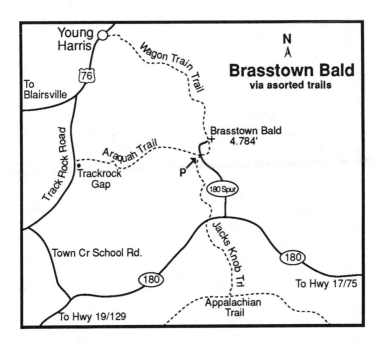

Young
Harris

N
Ʌ

To
Blairsville

76

Wagon Train Trail

Brasstown Bald
via asorted trails

Track Rock Road

Araquah Trail

Brasstown Bald
4.784'

Trackrock
Gap

P

180 Spur

Town Cr School Rd.

Jacks Knob Trl

180

180

To Hwy 17/75

To Hwy 19/129

Appalachian
Trail

Rabun Bald (4,696')

- via Bartram Trail & Bee Gum Gap Spur Trail
- Chattahoochee National Forest, GA

- Length: 3.0 miles round trip from lower parking area
          1.0 mile round trip from upper parking area
- Difficulty: moderate
- Overall elevation gain: approx. 1,000 feet from lower area

Majestic Rabun Bald is Georgia's second highest summit, and at 4,696 feet, looks down onto the scenic Rabun County resort of Sky Valley. Surpassed in height only by Brasstown Bald (4,784'), Rabun Bald offers a refreshingly different summit experience from that of its cousin to the west. Unlike Brasstown, Rabun Bald offers an experience of near solitude for its visitors. The combination of a complete lack of facilities and the difficulty in locating access routes combine to make Rabun Bald one of Georgia's best little-known peaks.

The Trail: Two relatively short options to Rabun Bald's summit are available. One is to begin at Bee Gum Gap, following a spur trail along an old roadbed. This path soon merges with the famous Bartram Trail and reaches the summit at mile 1.5. A quicker and easier route follows an old, bumpy gravel road through Bee Gum Gap up to a tiny parking area below the summit. The Bartram Trail continues climbing alongside this parking area, rising another 0.5 mile to the mountain's peak. Take your choice, but be aware that the gravel road leading to the upper parking area is extremely rough in spots. Besides, the walk will do you good! Both routes traverse beautiful, shady hardwood forests along Rabun Bald's cool northern slopes.

Above the upper parking area, the Bartram Trail snakes through a series of moderately steep switchbacks, gaining altitude rapidly through lush rhododendron thickets. The pathway straightens and flattens somewhat once it attains the ridgeline that makes up the summit, and soon emerges into the open bald atop the peak. Here, at the base of an old stone and wood observation deck, the Bartram Trail reaches a junction with the Three Forks Trail, merging from the east.

The old stone tower reaches about 20 feet into the air,

24

and places you well above the surrounding treeline. The term "360 degree panorama" was coined here, and terms such as "breathtaking" become sadly lacking. Dozens of rugged peaks and deep, forested valleys unfurl before you. Steep, rocky peaks in the Nantahalas to the north compete with rolling ridgelines to the east and south. Sky Valley lies nestled to the west. Truly this is a spot to linger and enjoy nature at its best. Rabun Bald is a real sleeper among Georgia peaks, and is definitely recommended to those wishing to escape the tourist crunch.

Directions: From Dillard, proceed north on Hwy 441 to GA Hwy 246. Turn right onto Hwy 246 and proceed 4.3 miles to the Sinclair station on the right and the sign directing you toward Sky Valley. Turn right here and drive 2.8 miles to the gravel road on your right. There is often a sign here - "Rabun Bald", but not always. Proceed up the gravel road 0.3 mile to Bee Gum Gap. Here, you will see the road continue straight ahead to the upper parking area, and the spur trail begins behind a vehicle-blocking mound of dirt. Take your pick.

Additional Hikes: Rabun Bald's summit can also be reached by the Three Forks Trail and the Bartram Trail from both north and south. The Three Forks Trail is a steep, challenging 6 mile round trip from FS 7 (Hale Ridge Road) to the east. The trail continues over 6 miles past FS 7 to the banks of the West Fork of the Chattooga River at scenic Three Forks. Many variations of entry and exit points can be considered. The Bartram Trail crosses FS 7 north of Rabun Bald, and runs 17 miles south to the Warwoman Dell Recreation Area just east of Clayton.

Rabun Bald

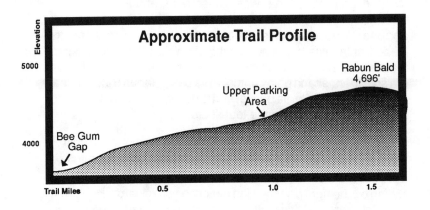

Approximate Trail Profile

Elevation

5000

Rabun Bald
4,696'

Upper Parking
Area

Bee Gum
Gap

4000

Trail Miles   0.5   1.0   1.5

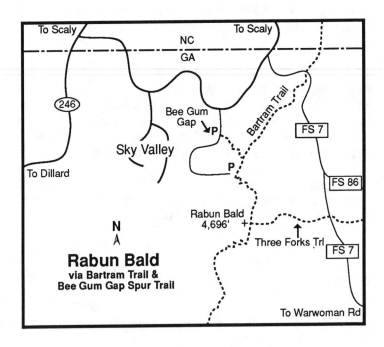

To Scaly   To Scaly

NC
GA

246

Bee Gum
Gap   P

Bartram Trail

FS 7

Sky Valley

To Dillard   P

FS 86

Rabun Bald
4,696'   +

N

Three Forks Trl   FS 7

Rabun Bald
via Bartram Trail &
Bee Gum Gap Spur Trail

To Warwoman Rd

Black Rock Mountain (3,640')

• via Tennessee Rock Trail
• Black Rock Mountain State Park, GA

• Length: 2.2 mile loop trail
• Difficulty: moderate
• Overall elevation gain: 400 feet

Black Rock Mountain State Park, Georgia's highest, contains several of the most visitor friendly overlooks in the entire Southern Appalachian chain. This 1500 acre park contains 6 peaks with elevations exceeding 3000 feet, and while it is not altogether uncommon to be able to drive within a short distance of a southern summit, few peaks are so easy to conquer.

Located along the steep southern-facing cliffs near the summit, the park's visitors center features the Black Rock overlook. This magnificent cliff face gazes some 1500 feet down onto the mountain town of Clayton, and features stunning views of nearby peaks such as Screamer and Tiger Mountain, as well as numerous additional peaks and the piedmont section of South Carolina beyond. Especially captivating sunrises can be captured from this overlook. The park features 3 additional overlooks - the Cowee and Blue Ridge overlooks along the main park entrance road, and the Nantahala overlook, located in the park camping area. Any visit to Black Rock Mountain State Park should include a visit to these convenient overlooks.

The Trail: The actual summit of Black Rock Mountain is due west and approximately 180 feet above the park visitor's center. This trail is normally reached via the popular Tennessee Rock Trail, a delightful 2.2 mile loop path. This interesting hike begins in a large gravel parking area located along the main park road, about halfway between the camping area turnoff and the visitor's center. Yellow blazes mark the route throughout, and it is recommended that visitors bear right at the first trail fork (this is the easier direction to follow). Among the features you will encounter along your nature walk are a beautiful hardwood forest and a thick, pungent stand of white pines.

Just beyond the white pine grove, a steep series of switchbacks takes you to the undulating ridgeline that is Black Rock Mountain's summit. The actual high point (3,640') is heavily wooded, and doesn't afford much sightseeing. Continue on several hundred yards and you will reach the Tennessee Rock Overlook, a bare, rocky undeveloped overlook featuring fantastic views of Germany and Wolffork Valleys, as well as the rugged peaks to the west and northwest. On clear days, distant summits such as Brasstown Bald are clearly visible from Tennessee Rock. If sunsets are what you're looking for, Tennessee Rock is your destination. Use caution here, however, as the cliff face below Tennessee Rock is sheer, and there is no railing to prevent visitor's from the dangerous drop.

The trail continues along the ridgeline from Tennessee Rock, and affords good views to either side of the mountain. After several hundred yards, the path begins a moderate descent back to the trailhead parking area.

For those unable to negotiate the 2.2 mile loop, a shortcut to Tennessee Rock and Black Rock's summit is available. Due to a shortage of parking and the hazards involved along this particular portion roadway, the park doesn't promote this route, but will normally oblige visitor's when asked. The shortcut involves hiking up a short, several hundred yard section of the Tennessee Rock trail, and is located about halfway between the visitors center and the park's cabins.

Directions: Drive north from Clayton on Highway 441 for 3 miles to Mountain City. Follow the signs and turn left onto the park entrance road. Follow for 3 miles to the park visitor's center for additional information.

Alternate Hikes: Black Rock Mountain State Park also features the James Edmonds Backcountry Trail (7.2 miles - moderate to difficult) and the Ada-Hi Falls Nature Trail (0.2 mile - steep climb) for those looking for additional challenges.

Black Rock Mountain

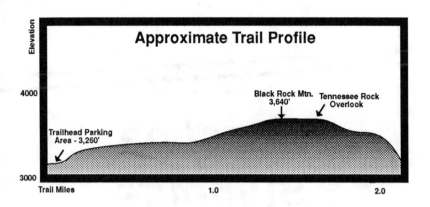

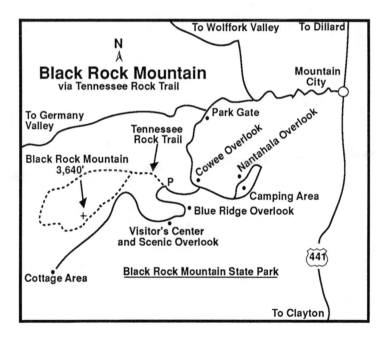

South Carolina Summits

Table Rock (3,157')
- via Table Rock Trail
- Table Rock State Park

- Length: approx. 6 miles round trip
- strenuous
- overall elevation gain: approx. 2,000 feet plus

      The scenic Foothills area of South Carolina contains several of the Southern Appalachians most interesting peaks. One of these, Table Rock, rises abruptly from the surrounding hills, soaring over 2,000 feet above the surrounding terrain. This peak, one of 2 exceeding 3,000 feet in the park, has been challenging the recreational hiker since the park was developed in the 1930's by the Civilian Conservation Corps. The Native Americans referred to this mountain as "The Stool", and you'll certainly need one after you tackle this summit. A visit to the historic park is a must, but carefully and honestly guage your stamina level before attempting the punishing hike up Table Rock.
      Table Rock State Park's trail system originates behind the park's nature center, and each hiker is required to register. Three separate trails begin here - the Pinnacle Mountain Trail (also a Foothills Trail access trail), Carrick's Creek Nature Trail, and the Table Rock Trail. Each trail is conveniently blazed, with the Table Rock Trail following red blazes throughout.

The Trail: The path to Table Rock initially follows the eastern loop of the Carrick's Creek Nature Trail. This delightful footpath meanders briefly past several beautiful cascades along Carrick's Creek and its tributaries before beginning the long ascent. The initial 2 miles of trail are relentlessly steep. The scenery is superb, though, so take advantage of any breaks to sightsee. One of the main attractions along the rugged trail is a mammoth boulder field on Table Rock's southern slope. As the trail traverses the boulder field, huge house-sized boulders and slabs crowd the path. This area alone may be worth visiting separately from the summit, and one could take their pick of good picnic spots here.
      Just past the boulderfield a small trailside shelter may be utilized for catching your breath or escaping any inclement weather which may have surprised you. A long straight ahead

grade soon arrives at a junction near mile 2.0 with a path veering over to Pinnacle Mountain. To the right, the Table Rock Trail continues, plateauing out for nearly half a mile. This relatively flat section is most welcome, but don't think all your work is over yet.

The steep western face of Table Rock is next, and contains the steepest and roughest sections of the trail. The narrow, rocky, and root laden path can be tricky here, and great caution should be exercised in wet conditions. Several areas of the path cross smooth, steep granite outcrops, making footing treacherous. After scrambling upwards for several hundred feet, the path emerges onto a broad, sloping granite outcropping known as "Governors Rock". At 2,920 feet, this overlook provides nice views westward to Pinnacle Mountain, with several rocky cliffs below.

The trail continues to climb further up the ridgeline before levelling again briefly. A sign announces "Table Rock Mountain - 3,124". A small, muddy spring surprisingly rises closeby. The mountain's highpoint - 3,157 feet - is still several minutes away, up one last scrambling climb! On top of Table Rock is a dense mixed forest with a good deal of underbrush. Several rocky overlooks lie along the mountain's sheer cliffs, and visitors should be extremely cautious when exploring the summit. The nearby ridgeline of Caesar's Head can be seen to the northeast. Distant Mt. Pisgah can also be seen under ideal conditions to the north.

Enjoy your stay atop Table Rock. The steep return trip to the nature center is hard on the knees and ankles. It is well worth noting that since the trail is long, hikers should carefully consider beginning their descent several hours before the onset of dusk. More than a few hikers have been forced to complete the final portions of this trail in the dark. If you meet the qualifications, you will definitely enjoy Table Rock Mountain.

Directions: Table Rock State Park is located on Hwy 11 about 16 miles north of Pickens, SC. Enter at either gate and drive along the main park road to the large parking area across from the nature center.

Alternate Hikes: As mentioned earlier, several other trails are available to hikers in the park. The Carrick's Creek Nature Trail makes a highly scenic 3 mile loop across the lower slopes of the mountain, passing numerous delightful cascades along the way. The trail to Pinnacle Mountain is considered by many to be the most difficult in the park, and leads past beautiful waterfalls and along several steep cliffs. A round trip hike to the summit is approximately 5 miles.

Another good summit vantage point is at Caesar's Head State Park, about 20 minutes northeast of Table Rock on Hwy 276. From the observation area along the cliffs, excellent profile views of Table Rock and surrounding Table Rock Lake are visible. Several good hiking trails can be found at Caesar's Head, including a 5 mile round trip hike to the stunning Raven Cliffs Falls, one of the tallest series of cascades in the South.

Table Rock

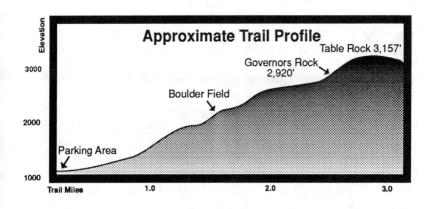

Approximate Trail Profile

Table Rock 3,157'

Governors Rock 2,920'

Boulder Field

Parking Area

Elevation

3000

2000

1000

Trail Miles   1.0   2.0   3.0

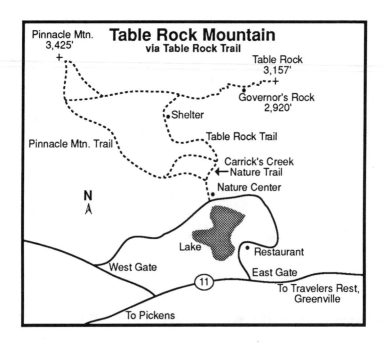

Table Rock Mountain
via Table Rock Trail

Pinnacle Mtn. 3,425'

Table Rock 3,157'

Governor's Rock 2,920'

Shelter

Table Rock Trail

Pinnacle Mtn. Trail

Carrick's Creek
Nature Trail

Nature Center

N

Lake

Restaurant

West Gate

East Gate

11

To Pickens

To Travelers Rest, Greenville

North Carolina Summits

Scaly Mountain (4,804')

• via Bartram Trail
• Nantahala National Forest, NC

• **Length: 3.0 miles round trip**
• **Difficulty: strenuous**
• **Overall elevation gain: approx. 1,050 feet**

The Scaly Mountain area of Southwestern North Carolina is known more as one of the southernmost ski areas in the Appalachians than as a hiking destination, yet the broad rocky summit of Scaly Mountain offers majestic views of nearby summits Osage Mountain and Rabun Bald to the south, as well as piedmont areas to the east. An often steep 1.5 mile path climbs over 1000 feet from NC 106 to the summit, with the majority of the path following a segment of the North Carolina Bartram Trail.

The trail to Scaly's summit begins across the street from the Osage Mountain vista. Wooden stairs initiate the hiker onto this portion of the yellow-blazed trail as it winds upward through the Nantahala National Forest. The initial 0.6 mile is very steep, and traverses a large area of young growth, the result of a recent burn. Approximately 0.4 mile up the trail, a short side path descends to a small ravine featuring a tiny but noisy splashing waterfall. The spot is shaded in thick rhododendron, and offers a good spot to catch one's breath. The trail continues upward, crossing the tiny rivulet just above the falls, and remains somewhat steep until joining an old roadbed near 0.6 mile. Bear right onto the road and begin a gradual ascent below the rocky mountain summit, visible through the forest canopy before you. Hike about 0.6 mile along the old rocky road until a spur trail appears on the left (the road levels off before the junction).

This spur trail winds about 0.3 mile through open forest, initially along level terrain. The several hundred foot climb to the summit ocurs along a series of easy switchbacks along the mountain's northeast slope. This final section traverses a large grove of gnarled oaks (I think one of these trees was in the movie "Poltergeist"), and some nice views of peaks to the north can be enjoyed in the leafless cooler months.

The Scaly Mountain summit, at an elevation 0f 4,804', is broad, rocky and features numerous open areas. Dense thickets of laurel choke the summit, and thick, rich mats of mosses and lichens cushion much of the rock face. The views to the south are spectacular, particularly of Georgia's Rabun Bald (4,696'). Glimpses of sparkling mountain lakes and nearby pastures can also be caught. On particularly clear days, the seemingly endless peaks stretching to the west seem to fade into the horizon. Take your time and explore among the numerous side paths across the summit. Chances are pretty good that you may have the entire summit to yourself.

Directions: From Highlands, NC, follow NC 106 south for 6 miles to the Osage Mountain vista (NOT the Blue Valley overlook). From Dillard, GA, follow GA 246 past Sky Valley, through the Scaly community, to the Osage Mountain vista. The trail to Scaly Mountain begins across the road from the overlook. Warning: drivers along this section of NC 106 are often caught up with sightseeing, and crossing the highway can truly be an adventure.

Scaly Mountain

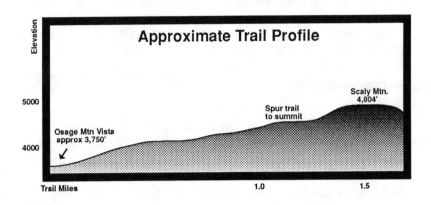

Approximate Trail Profile

Elevation

5000

4000

Osage Mtn Vista
approx 3,750'

Spur trail
to summit

Scaly Mtn.
4,804'

Trail Miles

1.0

1.5

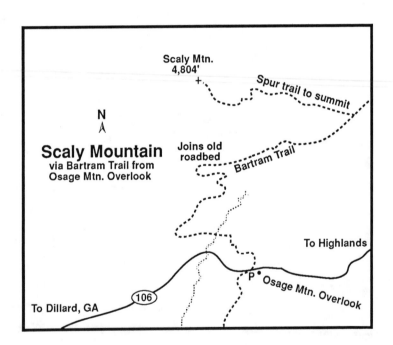

Scaly Mtn.
4,804'

Spur trail to summit

N

Scaly Mountain
via Bartram Trail from
Osage Mtn. Overlook

Joins old
roadbed

Bartram Trail

To Highlands

To Dillard, GA

106

P Osage Mtn. Overlook

Whiteside Mountain (4,930')

• via Whiteside Mountain National Recreational Trail
• Nantahala National Forest, NC

• **Length: 2 mile loop trail**
          3.5 miles including Devil's Courthouse spur trail
• **Difficulty: moderate**
• **Overall elevation gain: approx. 500 feet**

One of the Southern Appalachians most fascinating peaks, Whiteside Mountain, rises suddenly from the Nantahala National Forest, and features the highest sheer cliffs in the eastern United States. Appropriately named for its stark greyish-white granite cliffs, Whiteside has long attracted attention throughout history. Native Americans called Whiteside the "sitting down place" and often camped atop the table-like monolith during their travels.

The US Forest Service acquired the mountain in 1974, and now manages a 2 mile loop trail across the summit. This delightful pathway is now designated a National Recreational Trail and is a component of the National Trail System.

The Trail: Whiteside's loop trail begins in a large graveled parking area about 500 feet below the mountain's high point, and climbs gently northeast along an old, rocky roadbed. At one time this roadway ran to the top of the mountain. The old roadbed stretches along the shaded north face of the peak, and passes through mature hardwood groves and past impressive displays of native wildflowers.

Just before the 1 mile point, the path emerges into a clearing at the eastern tip of the mountain. Here, the trail turns sharply right and begins an easy ascent toward the summit. A spur trail drops from this clearing 0.75 mile down to the popular Devil's Courthouse area. This spur trail begins just east of the commemorative plaque in the clearing. If you are in reasonably good shape and not afraid of heights, this area may be worth exploring. A narrow, rough primitive path drops rather abruptly through dense undergrowth to the courthouse, losing all of the elevation that you have gained since leaving the parking area. Those wishing to venture down are rewarded with stunning views

39

of the headwaters region of the Chattooga River, Sapphire Valley, Chimneytop and Rock Mountain, among other scenic points. The Courthouse elevation is 4,485', almost 500 feet below Whiteside's elongated summit, and is surrounded on 3 sides by extremely dangerous sheer cliffs approaching 700 feet high! Visitor's must negotiate an overgrown path to a narrow arm of the mountain to reach the spire that makes up Devil's Courthouse. On top of this arm are several thousand square feet of level, rocky ground where one can relax and enjoy the views. It cannot be overstated that this area is primitive, and there are no railings or signs to warn foolish visitors of the dangers along the cliffs. Needless to say, use all common sense if you decide to visit Devil's Courthouse. If you have small children, you will want to avoid this side trip.

Back in the clearing at the head of the spur trail, the main pathway turns sharply right and begins an easy climb along the mountain's spectacular southern ridgeline. This 0.75 mile section hugs the rim of the highest sheer cliffs in the east. Dizzying views of the valley 2,000 feet below are visible from this entire section of trail. Lakes, homes and even fields are reduced to mere specks from atop the peak. The twin peaks of Chimneytop and Rock Mountain dominate the view to the east. Clear days offer distant views into the South Carolina piedmont.

At approximately mile 1.5, the small knob comprising Whiteside's highpoint is reached. The elevation 4,930' has been chiseled into the rock. Take your time and explore this section of trail along the cliff faces. Fencing allows you to hug the very edge of the cliffs, providing great photo opportunities! Good populations of red oak, birch, maple and fraser's magnolia exist atop the mountain, and may be overlooked due to the outstanding views.

While walking along the cliffs, keep a sharp eye out for the endangered Peregrine Falcon, which has been re-introduced to this area. These magnificent birds nest along the rocky cliffs, and can often be seen spiraling in the strong mountain updrafts. In order to help these birds repopulate, the Forest Service closes the cliffs to rock climbers and repellers during the nesting season.

From the mountain's highpoint, the trail begins a slight descent along Wildcat Cliffs before turning right and beginning a steep, switchbacking 0.25 mile drop to the parking area.

Directions: Whiteside Mountain is conveniently located 5 miles east of Highlands, and 5 miles west of Cashiers, off Hwy 64. Turn south onto Whiteside Mountain Road (1690) at the Macon/ Jackson County line and proceed to the parking area.

The view east from Whiteside's summit toward Chimneytop Mtn.

Whiteside Mountain

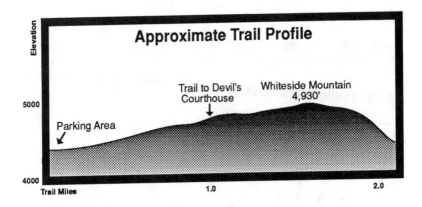

Approximate Trail Profile

Elevation

5000

4000

Trail Miles

1.0

2.0

Trail to Devil's Courthouse

Whiteside Mountain 4,930'

Parking Area

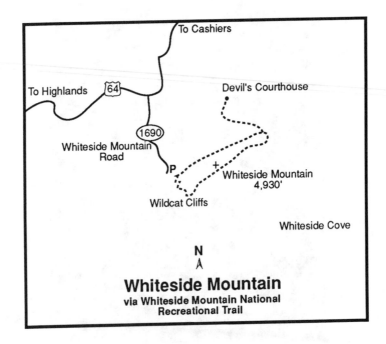

To Cashiers

To Highlands

64

Devil's Courthouse

1690

Whiteside Mountain Road

P

Whiteside Mountain 4,930'

Wildcat Cliffs

Whiteside Cove

N

Whiteside Mountain
via Whiteside Mountain National Recreational Trail

Yellow Mountain (5,127')
• via Yellow Mountain Trail
• Nantahala National Forest, NC

• **Length: 9.6 miles round trip**
• **Difficulty: strenuous**
• **Overall elevation gain: 800 feet overall, almost 2,000 feet in total climbing to summit.**

      Yellow Mountain is a relatively little-known summit that rises from the rugged escarpment region just north of Highlands, NC. The hike covers a great deal of varying terrain, and the trail profile undulates wildly over the 4.8 mile climb to the summit. The near 800 foot overall elevation gain does not accurately reflect the severe up-and-down nature of the trail, which totals almost 2,000 feet. Because of this, only experienced hikers in good physical condition should attempt this hike. Yellow Mountain is another one of those Southern Appalachian peaks that, because of the trail length and difficulty, you may get to enjoy all to yourself on occasion.

The Trail: This challenging trail begins in Cole Gap along Buck Creek Road. A metal signpost marks the trailhead. The initial 1 mile rises gently but steadily through alternating groves of rhodo-dendron, hardwoods, and massive hemlocks. Just beyond the 1 mile mark, a steep, switchbacking climb up Cole Mountain be-gins. After a short dip into a small gap, the trail then meanders straight ahead up and across the flat ridge of Shortoff Mountain. At this point, the trail has ascended approximately 700 feet since Cole Gap, which should have warmed you up sufficiently for things to come. Look for the flourescent tape atop Shortoff which marks a short side trail running out to a smooth granite overlook. This overlook gazes south over the serene plateau.

      Just past the 2 mile point, the trail begins a moderately steep prolonged descent from Shortoff along a severely eroded portion of the trail. At about mile 2.5, you will reach a fork, marked by the remains of a vandalized signpost. To the right, the path drops down to Norton Road. Continue straight ahead, following the path up slightly over Goat Knob. The path then drops rapidly down to mile 3.5, bottoming out in Yellow Mountain Gap, a full 900 feet below Shortoff's summit.

Beyond Yellow Mountain Gap, the final climb of the trail begins. The remaining 1,000 foot climb to Yellow Mountain's summit is moderate, but may be exaggerated in difficulty because of the previous climbing required just to get to this point. This portion of the trail is well laid, but several long straight-ahead grades are tiring.

The final 0.75 mile is up a broad ridge, and follows a severely eroded portion of trail. Less than 0.5 mile from the top, the path briefly parallels an old jeep road which winds to the tower atop Yellow Mountain. Unless fatigue has conquered you, this final 0.5 mile is fairly easy.

Yellow Mountain's summit is a thick heath bald, with rocky outcroppings scattered about. An old trashed observation tower still stands, though no ladder remains inside to provide access to the 2nd floor viewing area. The panorama from the top is truly spectacular. Excellent views of Whiteside Mountain to the southeast combine with views east into Sapphire Valley to create a postcard scene. The hulking mass of Rabun Bald is visible on the southern horizon. One can easily retrace the hike over Cole and Shortoff Mountains in the foreground. On the north side of the tower, rocky clearings allow impressive views into the Smokies and of peaks in the Nantahala range.

Enjoy your stay atop Yellow Mountain. The 4.8 mile return hike is every bit as challenging as the hike out.

Directions: From Highlands, follow Hwy 64 east from Highlands. After 3 miles, turn left onto Buck Creek Road and proceed 2.3 miles to Cole Gap. The trailhead is on the right side of the road, and a small dirt pulloff accomodates several vehicles. The trail begins by the metal signpost.

Yellow Mountain

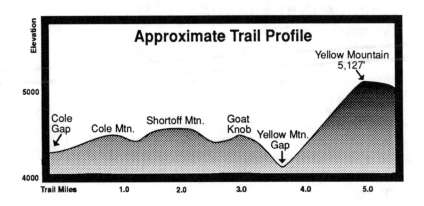

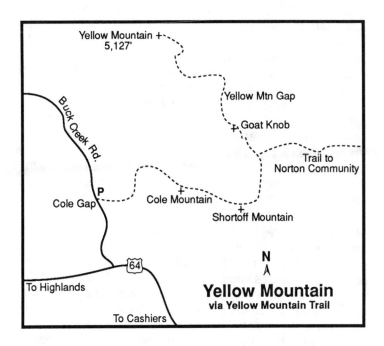

Chimneytop Mountain (4,618')

- via Chimneytop Trail
- High Hampton Inn

- Length: approx. 3 miles round trip
- Difficulty: strenuous
- Overall elevation gain: approx. 1200 feet

Note: This trail is on private property owned by the High Hampton Inn and Country Club. Anyone wishing to hike this trail MUST request permission at the Inn before beginning the hike.

Anyone travelling along Highways 64 or 107 through the resort town of Cashiers, NC has noticed the 2 rocky-sided peaks that guard the entrance to Sapphire Valley. These 2 picture-postcard summits, Rocky Mountain and Chimneytop Mountain are located on the grounds of of the historic High Hampton Inn and Country Club, and form an impressive backdrop for the resort. What many visitors to the area may not know, however, is that a remarkably scenic (and equally challenging) trail leads out to a gap between the 2 peaks, then splits and heads up to conquer both summits. Enchanting views of Cashiers Valley and Sapphire Valley can be enjoyed from the top, and dozens of rugged, rock-faced Southern Appalachian peaks fade into the distance from these peaks. The favorite, and higher, of the two is Chimneytop. For this reason Chimneytop is the peak that will be featured.

The Trail: The trail to Chimneytop's rocky summit is truly a Jekyll and Hyde path. Along its first mile, the shady pathway undulates gently northeast beneath beautiful, towering hemlocks, oaks and poplars, and passes through dense rhododendron thickets. The trail is generously wide, and negotiates numerous easy up and down grades, gradually ascending several hundred feet into the gap between Rocky Mountain and Chimneytop Mountain. From its very beginning at the inn, the twin peaks dominate the eastern sky, leaving no doubt as to your ultimate destination.

As the trail snakes into the narrow gap, hiker's will encounter a 4-way trail intersection. Straight ahead, the path drops downward for several steep miles into Sapphire Valley and emerges from the forest on the grounds of the Fairfield Sapphire Valley resort near the tennis center. The trail to the left climbs approximately 600 feet to the summit of Rocky Mountain, which overlooks beautiful High Hampton Inn and lake. If you decide to take the trail to the summit of Rocky Mountain, be aware of the sheer cliffs that drop down toward the lake - they can be quite dangerous. Back again at the intersection, the trail to the right is to our destination - Chimneytop, which is another 0.5 mile and 900 feet above the gap.

The blue-blazed trail changes personality markedly at the gap, and most would say for the worse. The previously forgiving stroll now becomes a tight, technical climb up the narrow, funnelling ridgeline. Steep switchbacks along the trail change direction quickly, and offer the hiker no real break from the harsh grade. If you have the ability to appreciate nature along the way, you will notice a constantly changing variety of pine, oak, rhododendron and laurel.

Several hundred trail yards below the summit, the path crosses several steep rocky outcroppings. The hike turns into a labored scramble over these rock faces, and mercifully terminates atop Chimneytop's appropriately named summit at approximately mile 1.5.

There is no shortage of good vantage points atop this deceptively large summit. The first good clearing you will encounter looks out south and west, and is usually littered with weary hikers sunning themselves. This overlook captures inspiring views of the valley, and especially of Whiteside Mountain's unusually steep profile. The actual highpoint of the peak is reached by continuing to follow the trail to the next rocky clearing, which looks north and west out over serene Sapphire Valley. This rough, pot-marked overlook contains a gold stake which marks the actual summit, and makes an incomparable picnic spot. A third overlook is reached by continuing along the shrinking trail which terminates on the northeast point of the peak. This enchanting, moss and lichen covered outcropping captures good views to the east. Any of these openings offer first-rate mountain panoramas, great scenery, and a deserved chance to rest! While you're struggling to make your climb to the top, try to resist the urge to fling your pack off the side of the mountain. Chimneytop Mountain is one of those peaks that will truly make you glad you did.

Directions: High Hampton Inn is located several miles south of Cashiers, NC along Highway 107. In order to prevent visitors from hiking the trail without authorization, directions to the trailhead must be obtained at the inn.

A visitor atop Chimneytop gazes into Sapphire Valley

Chimneytop Mountain

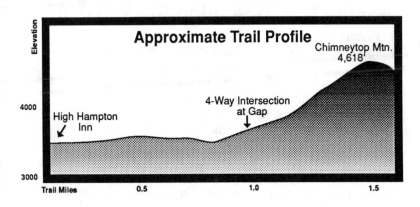

Approximate Trail Profile

Elevation

Chimneytop Mtn.
4,618'

4000

4-Way Intersection
at Gap

High Hampton
Inn

3000

Trail Miles   0.5   1.0   1.5

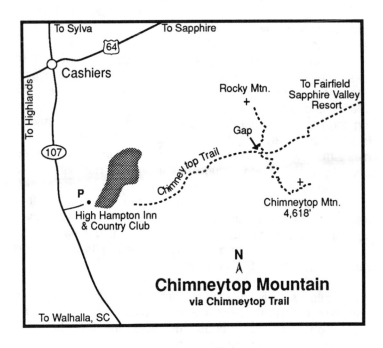

To Sylva   To Sapphire

64

Cashiers

To Highlands

Rocky Mtn.
+

To Fairfield
Sapphire Valley
Resort

Gap

107

Chimneytop Trail

P

+

High Hampton Inn
& Country Club

Chimneytop Mtn.
4,618'

N
Ʌ

Chimneytop Mountain
via Chimneytop Trail

To Walhalla, SC

Tennent Mtn. & Shining Rock (6,040')
• via various trails
• Pisgah National Forest / Shining Rock Wilderness, NC

• Length: 7.5 miles round trip to Tennent Mountain
           12 mile round trip to Shining Rock
• Difficulty: moderate to strenuous
• Overall elevation gain: approx. 1,000 feet

The strikingly beautiful and untamed Shining Rock Wilderness and ajoining areas of the Pisgah National Forest are home to some of the most strikingly unusual features in the Southern Appalachians. Numerous trails lace this high, rugged backcountry area and provide access to several peaks that exceed the 6,000 foot mark. Two of these peaks, Tennent Mountain and Shining Rock, are reached along established trails through this wilderness.

The area now comprising the Shining Rock Wilderness was once farmed by early settlers in the 1800's. Various logging interests and paper companies obtained the land in the early 1900's, and heavily logged the forests. Extensive networks of logging railroads laced the steep mountainsides, and some of today's trails wind along these old railbeds. The logging companies almost completely eliminated the vast stands of fir, spruce and virgin hardwoods. Huge forest fires in 1925 and 1942 permanently altered the forest vegetation. Today, instead of thick forests, vast fields and grassy balds abound. The area became part of the Pisgah National Forest in 1935, and in 1964 over 13,000 acres was permanently set aside as an original component of the National Wilderness System. The original designation was increased to 18,500 acres in 1984.

The Trails: A fairly complex system of trails runs through this portion of the Pisgah National Forest. Over a half dozen paths connect on Shining Rock Ledge, which spans the chasm between Tennent Mountain and Shining Rock.

The trail to Tennent Mountain and Shining Rock descends to and then crosses Yellowstone Prong before ascending Graveyard Ridge. This area is appropriately named, and is a good example of the type of vegetation found throughout the area.

Large open fields and scattered groves of heath vegetation create a strange, eerie atmosphere in this primitive wilderness setting.

After ascending several hundred feet up the open ridge, the trail begins to level somewhat along its 3 mile jaunt to Ivestor Gap. At approximately 2 miles, the path dips briefly and crosses the headwaters of Dark Prong. Directly in front of you, Tennent Mountain rises 600 feet. Unfortunately, the path is anything but direct, and still must cover nearly 2 undulating miles before reaching the peak's summit. Take advantage of the opportunities for sightseeing and visually explore this rich trail.

The path turns sharply west before climbing into Ivestor Gap and its multiple trail junction. From this junction, the Art Leob Trail (#146) winds south back to the parkway. Tennent's magnificent open summit lies approximately 0.75 mile south along this well-known pathway. Tennent Mountain is named for Dr. G. S. Tennent, a pioneer member of the Carolina Mountain Club. Consider this and other paths in the area if you would like to plan a route that takes you in a loop.

After returning to Ivestor Gap, continue north on the Leob Trail to Shining Rock Gap. This portion of the path undulates along the open Shining Rock Ledge, rising and falling across Grassy Cove Top, Flower Gap and Flower Knob. Views to the east and west of the open ridge are outstanding! To reach the wilderness area's namesake peak from Shining Rock Gap, veer onto the Old Butt Knob Trail (one must wonder exactly who or what this trail is named after) and climb several hundred feet across Shining Rock's southern face. The path runs just below the peak's highpoint, but you'll want to explore this fascinating wilderness summit. Shining Rock derives its picturesque name from a huge outcrop of white quartz that can be seen on its slopes from as far away as the parkway.

Views from the summit are as wild as the paths that brought you here. To the south, retrace your route over Shining Rock Ledge toward Tennent Mountain and Balsam Knob. To the west is Birdstand Mountain. Dominating the northern view is mammoth Cold Mountain.

Visitors should be sure to obtain a detailed forest service map of the area. The closest office is along Hwy 276 just north of Brevard. This type of good, topographical map is essential when visiting in a wilderness area as primitive and isolated as Shining Rock Wilderness. The multitude of trails lacing the region can be confusing even to seasoned veterans.

Directions: This trailhead to Tennent Mountain and Shining Rock begins in the Graveyard Fields parking area along the Blue Ridge Parkway. This section of the parkway is north of Brevard, NC, and west of Asheville. Follow the parkway to mile 418.8. The Graveyard Fields parking area is off to the northern side. The trailhead is marked. Be sure that you initially follow the Graveyard Ridge Trail, and not the Graveyard Fields Trail.

Tennent Mtn. & Shining Rock

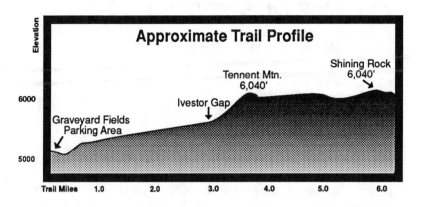

Approximate Trail Profile

Elevation

Shining Rock
6,040'

Tennent Mtn.
6,040'

Ivestor Gap

6000

Graveyard Fields
Parking Area

5000

Trail Miles   1.0   2.0   3.0   4.0   5.0   6.0

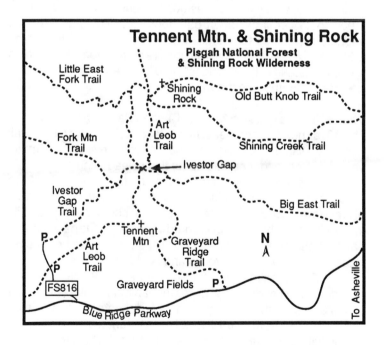

Tennent Mtn. & Shining Rock
Pisgah National Forest
& Shining Rock Wilderness

Little East
Fork Trail

+ Shining
Rock

Old Butt Knob Trail

Fork Mtn
Trail

Art
Leob
Trail

Shining Creek Trail

Ivestor Gap

Ivestor
Gap
Trail

Big East Trail

P

Tennent
Mtn

+

Graveyard
Ridge
Trail

N

Art
Leob
Trail

P

FS816

Graveyard Fields

P

Blue Ridge Parkway

To Asheville

Cheoah Bald (5,062')

• **via Appalachian Trail**
• **Nantahala National Forest, NC**

• **Length: 8.6 miles round trip**
• **Difficulty: strenuous**
• **Overall elevation gain: approx. 1,900 feet**

      Cheoah Bald is known primarily to Appalachian Trail thru-hikers as one in a series of rugged Cheoah Mountain Range peaks. Cheoah Bald's fascinating summit provides one of the very best panoramas in the Southern Appalachians. The rewards of conquering the summit carry a hefty price. The 4.3 mile hike up Cheoah Bald is challenging, exhilarating and exhausting. This is definitely not a hike for novices or small children. Do not let the 1,900 foot overall elevation gain fool you. This path's profile vaguely resembles someone's EKG, with the overall climb in the 2,500 foot range. The view from the crest has been described as the "Grandstand of the Smokies", and is generally considered as one of the South's finest panoramas.

The Trail: The quickest route to Cheoah Bald is via the Appalachian Trail heading southeast from Stecoah Gap. The official trail distance is listed at 4.3 miles. By the time you arrive at the summit, you'll have second thoughts about this mileage figure.

      The Appalachian Trail wastes no time in climbing from Stecoah Gap, rapidly gaining several hundred feet along a series of steep switchbacks. The path levels high above the gap, and its initial mile skips through a deep hardwood forest and past several narrow boulderfields. The path crosses these slide areas over moss and lichen covered rocks and boulders.

      At approximately 1.0 mile, the trail gains the crest of a high ridge and heads east toward Cheoah Bald. Take advantage of this and any other level ground you encounter along this hike - it is very rare. From mile 1.5 to 2.4 the path undulates wildly. The path initially drops several hundred feet from the high ridge down a steep grade into a small gap. No sooner do you reach the bottom than you immediately begin a tiring, straight-ahead ascent up the next steep ridge. It's somewhat disheartening on a summit hike to lose precious altitude that you must regain, yet Cheoah

Bald is one of those frustrating peaks. This trail burns a lot of calories before you even begin the real ascent. At the eastern end of this ridge, Cheoah Bald rises almost due east, still almost 3 trail miles distant.

The path drops lazily from the ridge at mile 2.I, and descends along a series of switchbacks into Locust Gap at mile 2.4. This descent passes through a section of young, thin growth in an area that appears to have been clear-cut some years past. Tall, shady hardwoods have been supplanted with thick under-growth and shrub vegetation. Locust Gap provides a good resting point, and a 200 yard long spur trail leads to a good natural water source.

The remaining 1.9 miles is very strenuous, and almost totally uphill. The path narrows in many areas, almost blocked by recent plant growth. The trail is quite rocky and root-laden, and normal walking can become quite tricky. A prolonged series of switchbacks pushes your ascent harder near the top. These last 2 miles from Locust Gap may seem more like 20 if you are not accustomed to such grades. Take frequent breaks, drink plenty of fluids, and push on!

The long narrow ridgeline comprising Cheoah Bald's summit is reached at mile 4.3. The mountain's high point measures 5,062 feet, and is noted by an inconspicuous wooden sign. The first thing newcomers will notice is the broad, rich meadow on the summit's southern flank. This meadow, perhaps 5 or more acres in size, offers superb open views of dozens of Nantahala Range peaks to the south. Directly below but out of sight is the popular Nantahala River. The meadow's unusual openness creates a stark but beautiful contrast with the thickly forested slopes, and creates a near perfect setting for camping or picnicing.

On the north side of the trail, several short paths lead out to rocky northern overlooks. These relatively small vantage points seem to gaze out over the entire southwestern Smokies Range. Peaks such as Thunderhead Mountain, Gregory Bald and Clingman's Dome rise majestically to the north. In the valley below, the town of Stecoah lies silently nestled among the rolling ridges. To your left, one can retrace a great deal of the ascent that brought you to this spectacular place. Then again, don't think about the ascent. Why dwell on negatives in a place like this?

Directions: To reach the Appalachian Trail in Stecoah Gap, head west along NC Hwy 28 from Stecoah, NC. Proceed several miles, then turn left onto Hwy 143, which heads toward Robbinsville. Proceed 1.7 miles to Stecoah Gap. The Appalachian Trail crosses the highway in the gap. Parking is in a small lot along the left (eastern) shoulder. The hike begins on the eastern side of the road behind the trail sign.

Cheoah Bald

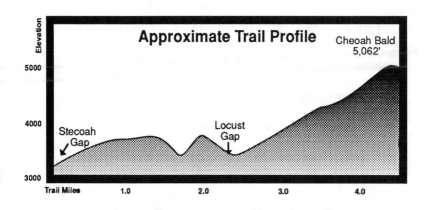

Approximate Trail Profile

Cheoah Bald
5,062'

Elevation

5000

4000

Stecoah
Gap

Locust
Gap

3000

Trail Miles   1.0   2.0   3.0   4.0

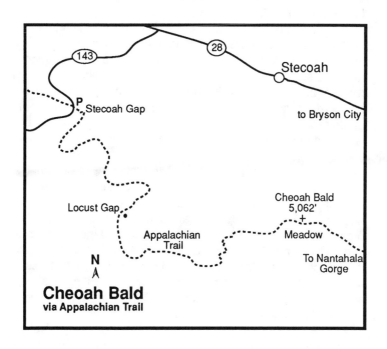

143

28

Stecoah

P Stecoah Gap

to Bryson City

Locust Gap

Cheoah Bald
5,062'
+
Meadow

Appalachian
Trail

To Nantahala
Gorge

N

Cheoah Bald
via Appalachian Trail

Standing Indian Mountain (5,499')

- **via Appalachian Trail**
- **Nantahala National Forest, NC**

- **Length: 5 miles round trip**
- **Difficulty: moderate**
- **Overall elevation gain: approx. 1200 feet**

"The Place Where Man Stood" is the Native American translation of Standing Indian Mountain, the tallest peak in the rugged Nantahala Mountain Range. This popular peak lies along the famous Appalachian Trail just north of the Georgia/North Carolina line, and has been attracting large numbers of day-hikers and thru-hikers for years.

The most convenient way to visit this spectacular ridge-line summit is via the 2.5 mile segment of Appalachian Trail that winds upward from Deep Gap. The grade is surprisingly moderate for a summit of this elevation, though the climb is approximately 1200 feet. The welcome combination of old roadbed and modern trailway give hiker's a George Bush type path - kinder and gentler. Compared to other sections in the Nantahalas, this hike is almost too easy.

The Trail: From Deep Gap, the white-blazed Appalachian Trail climbs gently but consistently over a trailbed littered with roots and rocks. A narrow log bridge crossing a small ravine is negotiated 0.3 mile from the gap, and should not prevent any problems. Use care, though, as bridges of this type can become very slippery in wet weather. Just less than one mile from the gap, the trail passes an Appalachian Trail shelter on the left. Besides offering a good, sheltered nights sleep, a small but noisy stream alongside the shelter provides dependable water (and a good source of relaxation for campers).

Beyond the shelter, the trail climbs moderately. Look for several trail changes, as portions of the path have been moved slightly. The path continues to alternate between old roadway and regular trail along broad, looping sections until within 1 mile of the summit. This final portion becomes somewhat steeper, with numerous switchbacks carrying the trail yet higher. You will know you are nearing the summit when the trail burrows through several thick groves of native rhododendron.

The steep gradient slackens considerably before levelling below the summit ridgeline, which runs almost 1.5 miles. The trail continues for several hundred yards almost sidewalk flat until the junction with the blue-blazed summit spur trail. This short trail heads off to the right, winding for several hundred yards through heath bald vegetation before emerging in a small clearing atop Standing Indian's summit. This clearing is the site of an old observation tower, now long dismantled. The rocky surface in the clearing still bears the scars of structures past. Numerous firerings attest to this locations' popularity among campers.

This clearing offers perhaps the best vistas atop the mountain. Views to the south and west are far-reaching. Little Bald rises before you to the south, while Big Scaly features prominently to the west. It is especially interesting to gaze south, across the Tallulah River watershed, towards Tate City, the tiny valley community just across the Georgia line. The southern slopes of Standing Indian give rise to the once mighty Tallulah, now silenced by a string of dams across Georgia's Rabun County.

Directions: from Franklin, NC, take Highway 64 west. Proceed through the rocky gap cut through the mountains. Proceed past the Macon/Clay county line. Approximately 0.3 mile past the county line, 4.5 miles west of the cut, turn left onto FS 71. Proceed along FS 71 for 5.9 miles to Deep Gap. Park here and follow the Appalachian Trail east from the gap.

Alternate Hikes: The Standing Indian area is laced with dozens of miles of interesting, varied trails. The mountain is surrounded with pathways, some making the strenuous climb from the Tate City area in Georgia. Check with the local Forest Service office for detailed maps of these trails.

Standing Indian Mountain

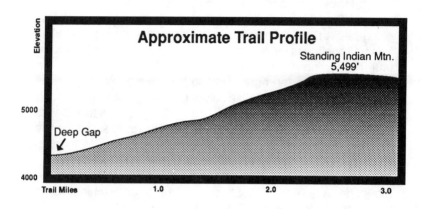

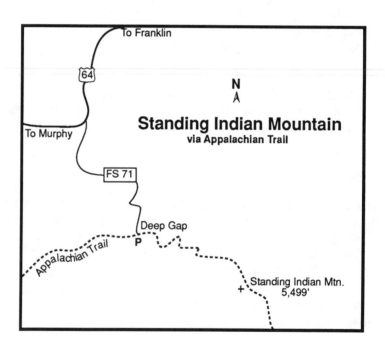

A lone hiker enjoying the view from Black Rock Mountain's
Tennessee Rock overlook.

Looking Glass Rock

- via **Looking Glass Rock Trail**
- **Pisgah National Forest, NC**

- **Length: 6.2 miles round trip**
- **Difficulty: strenuous**
- **Overall elevation gain: approx. 1700 feet**

     The most popular hiking trail in the Pisgah Ranger District is the highly scenic path that winds up the steep southeastern slopes of rugged Looking Glass Rock. Looking Glass is one of the South's more interesting summits, and though only 3,969 feet in elevation, has gained notereity due to the extremely steep, exposed granite slopes that are visible across this region. Anyone travelling along US 276 between the Cradle of Forestry and Brevard cannot help but notice the smooth, sheer cliffs rising abruptly from the forest. What they may not know, however, is that an excellent trail stretches to the summit, allowing sublime views to the north and west.

The Trail: The Looking Glass Rock Trail begins along FS 475, 0.4 mile west of Hwy 276. A metal stake denotes the trailhead in a small parking area along the right shoulder. This trail ascends 3.1 rugged miles, rising 1700 feet before attaining the summit. Pacing yourself is very important. In years past, the trail was much steeper and much more strenuous, though shorter. The route has been re-laid since, making this unusual summit open to almost any level hiker in good physical condition.

     The trail rises gently through its first mile, following yellow blazes through a mature, open hardwood forest. Flat, elongated switchbacks allow the hiker to enjoy the surroundings and warm up for the steeper grades ahead. A great deal of the first mile loops alongside, but well above, a serene, splashing brook. The noisy steam is strewn with moss covered rocks and lush undergrowth. Perhaps noticeable by now is the complete lack of the smooth, exposed granite that is the Looking Glass Rock trademark. Unlike the other 3 slopes, this southeastern approach burrows through a forest almost void of exposed rock. In several areas, one can gaze downward over previously walked sections of the looping trail.

The second mile is perhaps the trail's toughest, as the numerous switchbacks become tighter, steeper and relentless. The forest becomes mixed with conifers, rhododendron and laurel, and the path becomes increasingly rocky and root-laden. It is only your imagination that rocks and roots increase in size and frequency as the trail becomes more difficult! In several areas, as the trail turns through the switchbacks, glimpses of the sheer eastern face become visible through the forest canopy.

Beyond the rugged second mile, the path mercifully straightens out and the grade lessens greatly, providing a much needed break. The remaining several hundred vertical feet to the summit require over 1 mile to reach, making for a forgiving climb. The hardest work is now behind, yet the narrow, rocky nature of the path still requires great care.

At approximately mile 2.5, the trail passes a smooth, open outcropping to the left. Paths lead down from here to steep, slippery slopes on the mountain's southern side. A sign appropriately denounces throwing objects from this area, as it is one of the popular rock climbing areas of Looking Glass Rock. Beyond this area, the trail turns north, climbing slightly to the top of the ridge. Once astride the ridge, the path turns tightly west, and begins the final gentle climb to the summit.

The actual highpoint of Looking Glass Rock is a disappointment, as a tall grove of shade trees prevents the anticipated sweeping vistas. Numerous good camping spots lie beneath the shady hardwoods. Do not fret, though, as the path continues across the summit, then begins to drop rapidly. Several hundred yards later, the trail emerges into the open daylight along the peak's sheer northern cliffs.

This is a dangerous area, and no railings exist to prevent the curious or foolish from venturing too far down the slippery rockface. Needless to say, those not exercising common sense and safety could end up over 1000 feet down in a big hurry. Be content to enjoy the magnificent view from the relative safety along the treeline here.

Stretching before you atop Looking Glass Rock is an outstanding string of scenery. The Blue Ridge Parkway winds high above you to the northwest. Mt Pisgah lies almost due north, as do the Pink Beds, in the foreground. The view must simply be seen to be appreciated, and with the 3.1 mile climb behind you now, you will have definitely earned it.

Directions: Follow Highway 276 from just east of Brevard, north for just over 4 miles. Turn left onto FS 475 (Fish Hatchery Road) and proceed 0.4 mile to the small parking area on the right.

Alternate Hike: An alternate trail to Looking Glass Rock is found on the mountain's western flank. This trail originates in the Slick Rock Falls cove, off FS 475-B. Details on this trail can be obtained at the Pisgah Ranger Station on Hwy 276.

Additional Area Attractions: This portion of the Pisgah National Forest is rich in outdoor beauty and attractions. Within minutes of Looking Glass Rock are such natural attractions as Looking Glass Falls, Moore Cove Falls, the Cradle of Forestry, the Fish Hatchery and the Blue Ridge Parkway. Scores of miles of hiking trails lace the area. Visit the Pisgah Ranger Station for more details.

The view from Looking Glass Rock - northwest face

Looking Glass Rock

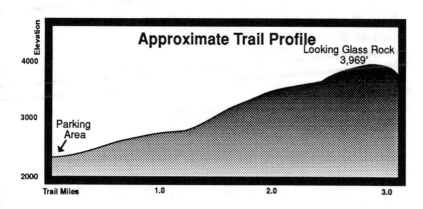

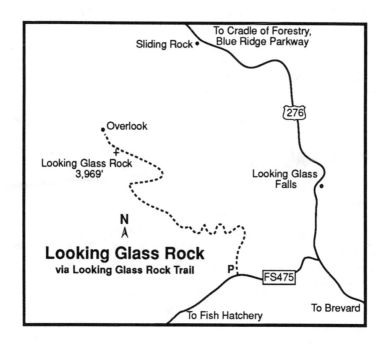

Looking Glass Rock
via Looking Glass Rock Trail

Mt. Pisgah (5,721')

• via Mt. Pisgah Trail
• Pisgah National Forest, NC

• **Length: 3.0 miles round trip**
• **Difficulty: moderate**
• **Overall elevation gain: approx. 900 feet**

Named for the Biblical peak from which Moses first looked out over the Promised Land, this easily conquered summit rises majestically from the surrounding Pisgah National Forest. This popular peak is conveniently located along the Blue Ridge Parkway just west of Asheville, NC. The pathway's relatively short length (1.5 miles to the summit) and close proximity to such a heavily traveled roadway combine to make Mt. Pisgah a favorite among southern summits.

The Trail: The trail to Pisgah's narrow summit begins in the Mt. Pisgah parking area. An information board states the one-way distance as 1.5 miles - some publications state 1.3. From the parking area, the conical summit looms tantalizingly close to the northwest. The summit is unmistakable - just look for the unsightly TV tower that dominates the peak.

The initial 0.8 mile meander almost sidewalk flat through a pleasant forest of delightful, mixed hardwoods. Thousands of rocks litter the path, creating a natural obstacle course for your feet. Natural grasses, mosses, rhododendrons and laurels combine to create an enchanting stroll.

The real work begins beyond 0.8 mile, as the trail bends west and begins an easy, initially gradual ascent along a narrow ridgeline. Several natural clearings allow overlooks to the north of the ridge, revealing highly scenic valleys. Beyond 1.0 mile, the trail becomes noticeably steeper and quite rocky. As the path negotiates the steep southern face of Mt. Pisgah, you will undoubtedly feel the urge to rest and catch your breath. Trail planners have thoughtfully (and mercifully) constructed several benches along this section to accomodate you heavy breathers.

After what may seem like dozens of never-ending switchbacks, the steep ascent moderates somewhat before depositing the trail into a typical Southern Appalachian bald near the summit.

This bald consists of choking groves of gnarled mountain laurels and twisted, grotesque oaks. The mountain's summit is very small, and thoroughly dominated by a large television transmitting tower. A small viewing deck provides truly outstanding panoramic vistas from the top.

To the northeast, Asheville's skyline can be clearly seen, set among the backdrop of spectacular distant summits. The picturesque Shining Rock Wilderness lies to the southwest, and points due south lie in the ajoining areas of the Pisgah National Forest. Directly below you to the south, you should be able to clearly pick out your vehicle in the Mt. Pisgah parking area. The trail and summit can become quite crowded during peak seasons, so plan your visit accordingly.

Directions: The Mt. Pisgah Trail begins in the Mt. Pisgah parking area, located between milepost 407 and 408 on the Blue Ridge Parkway. This section of the parkway is located west of Asheville. The closest access route is via Hwy 276 north of Brevard, NC. Enter the parking area and proceed to the dead-end. The trail begins beyond the information board.

Alternate Hikes: This particular area of the Pisgah National Forest is a hiker's delight. Other short walks or hikes can be undertaken from the Mt. Pisgah parking area. A short walk leads to the Buck Springs Overlook, and a junction with the Shut-In Trail runs through the parking area. Dozens of trails with hundreds of miles of all skill levels are available from points along Hwy 276 just south of the parkway. Additional details are available at the Pisgah Ranger Station on Hwy 276 just north of Brevard.

Mt. Pisgah

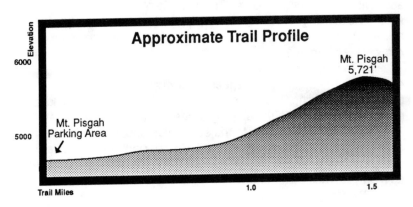

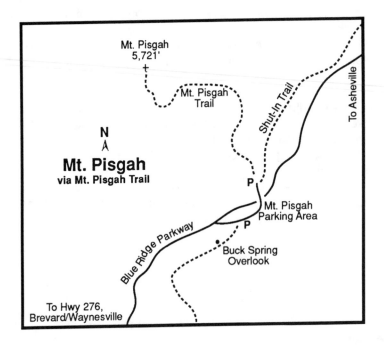

Mt. Mitchell (6,684')

- via various trails
- Mt. Mitchell State Park, NC

- Length: quickest route several hundred yards
- Difficulty: easy
- Overall elevation gain: approx. 100 feet

The tallest point in eastern North America, Mt. Mitchell, rises 6,684' above sea level. This ancient peak, the featured attraction in 1,677 acre Mt. Mitchell State Park, is part of the rugged Black Mountain chain, eastern America's highest range. Six of the ten highest eastern North American peaks are found in this relatively small range, and it is only appropriate that the tallest peak is also one of the easiest to visit in all of the south. North Carolina Highway 128 winds for several miles up the mountain from the Blue Ridge Parkway, and enters the park, North Carolina's oldest (founded in 1915), several miles south of the summit.

The early history of Mt. Mitchell makes fascinating reading. Unfortunately, space dictates the amount of details we can include here, but we'll try to relate the highpoints.

In 1835, a science professor from the University of North Carolina, Dr. Elisha Mitchell, visited the area to perform calculations on various peaks of the Black Mountains. Back in the early 1800's, many thought North Carolina's Grandfather Mountain was the region's tallest. Mitchell's earliest calculations put the highest of the Black Mountains at 6,476 feet. Subsequent visits in 1838 and 1844 led to a revised elevation of 6,672 feet - off by only 12 feet from today's confirmed measurement - amazing, considering the technology of the day.

Controversy about the reported elevations flared again in the 1850's, when Thomas Clingman (of Clingman's Dome fame), a former student of Dr. Mitchell, disagreed over Dr. Mitchell's findings. In 1857, Dr. Mitchell returned to the Black Mountains to verify his calculations and tragically fell to his death from a cliff above a waterfall. The highest of the Black Mountain peaks was named in his honor in 1858. Dr. Mitchell was originally buried in Asheville, but was appropriately entombed atop his peak several years after his death.

Mt. Mitchell's earliest recorded history included visits in

the 1780's by noted French botanist Andre Michaux and Englishman John Fraser. The renowned Fraser Fir was named after John Fraser.

The summit of Mt. Mitchell offers almost surreal panoramas of the surrounding Pisgah National Forest. From the mountain's elevation, which exceeds one mile, the view is somewhat like what you would gain from an airplane.

The mountain's high point features a stone observation tower, which reaches high above the surrounding trees. Photoplaques spaced around the tower railings aid visitors in identifying points both near and far. Many interesting features are pointed out on the ridgelines before you, including the noticeable railbeds of the old lumber company railroads from the early 1900's. Ridgeline views north and south are especially scenic. Visitors can easily follow the high ridgeline north over Mt. Craig, Big Tom, Balsam Cove and Cattail Peak, all exceeding 6,500 feet.

On a sad note, Mt. Mitchell, like Clingman's Dome and other high altitude Southern Appalachian peaks, has had a severe reduction in the number of Fraser Fir and Red Spruce trees over the last decade. Scientists debate the cause, but certainly not the result. Blame ranges from air pollution (acid rain/ acid fog) to invading insects. If it has been 10 years since your last visit to Mt. Mitchell, be ready for quite a shock. Thousands of these previously majestic fir and spruce trees now either lie broken upon the rocky slopes, or stand stark against the sky. We can only hope that researchers will make a definite determination soon, and that citizens will force the appropriate agencies to respond accordingly.

The Trails: Even though the summit of Mt. Mitchell is easily attainable via automobile, this high altitude park features numerous other hiking trails of varying levels of difficulty. These trails generally radiate from the summit, and offer something for every visitor. The following is a quick listing - trail details can be obtained from the park office.
• Old Mitchell Trail: moderately difficult - 2 miles
• Mt. Mitchell Trail: difficult - 6 miles - 3600 foot elevation gain, runs from Black Mountain Campground to summit
• Balsam Trail: easy - .0.75 mile nature trail
• Camp Alice Trail: strenuous - 0.75 mile
• Deep Gap Trail: moderately difficult - 6 miles

Directions: Mt. Mitchell State Park is located approximately 33 miles northeast of Asheville. Take the Blue Ridge Parkway to Hwy 128. Highway 128 proceeds several miles up the mountain into the park. Continue straight ahead to the summit parking area.

Note: Like many other high-altitude Southern Appalachian peaks, Mt. Mitchell experiences severe conditions, especially in the winter. The park may be closed during periods of ice and snow. Call (704) 675-4611 for further information.

Mt. Mitchell's observation tower with Dr. Mitchell's tomb in the foreground.

Mt. Mitchell

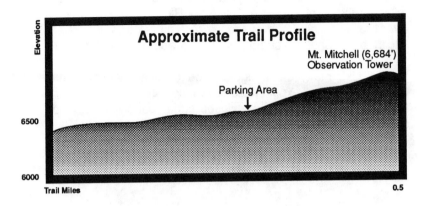

Approximate Trail Profile

Elevation

Mt. Mitchell (6,684')
Observation Tower

Parking Area

6500

6000

Trail Miles

0.5

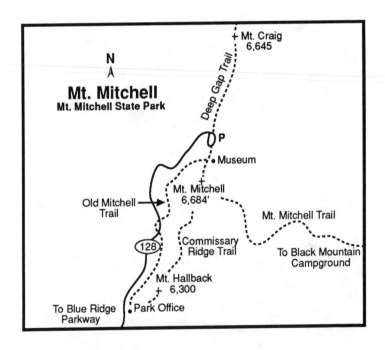

N

Mt. Mitchell
Mt. Mitchell State Park

Deep Gap Trail

+ Mt. Craig
6,645

P

• Museum

Old Mitchell
Trail

+ Mt. Mitchell
6,684'

Mt. Mitchell Trail

128

Commissary
Ridge Trail

To Black Mountain
Campground

Mt. Hallback
+ 6,300

To Blue Ridge
Parkway

• Park Office

Grandfather Mountain (5,964')

• **via Grandfather Trail**
• **Grandfather Mountain, NC**

• **Length: 4.4 miles minimum round trip**
• **Difficulty: strenuous and dangerous**
• **Overall elevation gain: approx. 600 feet**

Grandfather Mountain is truly one of the South's most magnificent and unusual peaks. This rugged summit rises high above scenic Linnville, NC, offering something rewarding for each and every visitor. This popular mountain is one of North Carolina's most visited attractions, and features panoramic views that are unsurpassed in the Southern Appalachians. This privately owned natural resource has been carefully developed and managed to encourage casual tourism, yet offers outdoors afficionados a challenging wilderness experience. The park's tremendous popularity is due partially to its prominent location along the ever-popular Blue Ridge Parkway. In fact, one of the parkway's most outstanding man-made features - the Linn Cove Viaduct - runs along Grandfather Mountain's southern slopes.

The Park: Grandfather Mountain posseses a unique combination of wild areas and nature-oriented attractions. Visitors not interested in hiking can enjoy splendid mountain scenery set among the park's natural beauty. Numerous excellent picnic areas lie along the main park road, just begging for use. Several developed yet rugged overlooks also beckon to beauty-starved visitors. Of special note is the new Grandfather Mountain Nature Museum and Visitor Center. This impressive structure houses a first class collection of naturalist exhibits ranging from wildlife to the weather. A cozy theatre presents professional films produced on location. The building also houses a gift shop and restaurant. On the grounds next to the nature museum, a wildlife habitat area has been constructed. This carefully planned area features habitats for black bear, deer, cougar and eagles, and has been meticulously constructed in order to impact the mountain as little as possible.

Automobiles may drive well up the mountain to the famous and seemingly timeless "mile high swinging bridge".

73

Here on the mountain's western flank, the pedestrian bridge spans a narrow chasm between the main ridgeline and an isolated rocky knob. This landmark attraction has been thrilling tourists for years. Postcard vistas can be captured from this easily accessed area. A smaller, somewhat older visitors center rests in the large open lot atop this western flank, and serves as the main parking area for Grandfather Mountain hikers.

The Trails: The "other side" of Grandfather Mountain is a true wilderness experience. The Grandfather Mountain backcountry offers over 3,000 acres of rugged, challenging wilderness. Miles of trails, most accessible from the swinging bridge parking area, reach across the mountain's treacherous, rocky ridgeline. This area has been designated a North Carolina Natural Heritage Area, and two of the nine trails here have been designated as National Recreational Trails. The area atop the ridgeline is for advanced hikers. Grandfather Mountain is one of the South's most rugged peaks, and exposes hikers to a wide variety of severe, sometimes life-threatening conditions. This is no place for beginners or the faint of heart.

The most popular route to the mountain's highpoint, Calloway Peak (5,964') is via the rugged Grandfather Trail. This arduous but thrilling trail crosses 5,939 foot Macrae Peak along the way, and sports Grandfather Mountain's infamous ladder climbs along sheer, rocky cliffs. If you are at all queasy about heights, avoid this section at all costs. The scenery all along this challenging trail is truly inspiring. For those not quite up to the ladder climbs, the 0.8 mile long Underwood Trail skirts around the sheer southwestern face of Macrae Peak before rejoining the Grandfather Trail east of the peak.

These trails allow hikers to enjoy Grandfather Mountain at is incomparable best. Beautiful fir and spruce compete with a staggering variety of rock faces to create one of the South's most scenic summits. Space limitations severely limit what a guide like this can tell you about such a beautiful area, but additional information can be obtained free of charge by writing the following:

Grandfather Mountain
Linville, NC 28646

A detailed trail map is available free of charge.

Please be aware that since Grandfather Mountain is privately owned, an admission fee must be charged to all visitors. Additionally, hikers must pay a daily trail-use fee. Proper permits

MUST be obtained before embarking on any hike. Permits are required even if you depart from one of the other trailheads accessing Grandfather Mountain trails. The park has an extensive list of regulations concerning backcountry trail use. These regulations are printed on the free trail map. These rules have been put into effect to protect both you and the fragile summit's ecosystems. Please obey all rules and regulations.

Directions: Grandfather Mountain is located several miles northeast of Linville, NC. Proceed from Linville along Hwy 221. The park gate will be on the left, and is unmistakably marked by a mammoth sign. The Blue Ridge Parkway runs along the peak's southern slopes. Turn west onto Hwy 221 from the parkway and proceed to the entrance on the right.

The famous mile-high swinging bridge, with Grandfather Mountain's Macrae Peak in the background.

Grandfather Mountain

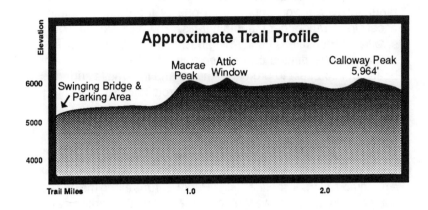

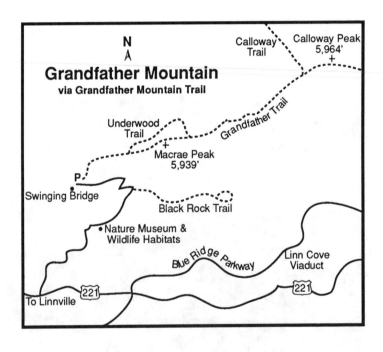

Smoky Mountain Summits

Mt. LeConte (6,593')

- via Appalachian Trail / Boulevard Trail / Alum Cave Trail
- Great Smoky Mountains National Park, TN

- **Length:** 13 mile minimum via this route
- **Difficulty:** strenuous
- **Overall elevation gain:** approx. 1500 ft. from Newfound Gap
  approx. 2800 feet from Alum Cave Trailhead

Mt. LeConte is a summit of superlatives. There are precious few Appalachian peaks - north or south - that can rival this summit in size, grandeur, vistas, or interesting features. It is not only one of the Southern Appalachians tallest mountains, but is also one of the region's steepest as well. The long ridgeline that comprises LeConte's summit features several excellent vantage points, both offering truly exceptional vistas.

This spectacular peak is named for Professor Joseph LeConte, a native Georgian who was a passionate hiker out west with the Sierra Club. The peak has a long and fascinating history - unfortunately too long for this guidebook. Sources at the park can steer you in the right direction for this type of information.

Even though visiting Mt. LeConte via hiking is long and difficult, the mountaintop is rarely a place of solitude. Day hikers, overnight campers (bunking in the 12 man LeConte shelter) and visitors lodging in the rustic LeConte Lodge share the LeConte experience. No one seems to mind too much, though, as there is a lot of mountain to go around.

The Trails: An entire book could be written about this peak's challenging hiking trails, and the following information should be considered only to whet your appetite.

Mt. LeConte can be accessed along numerous trails seemingly from every direction. Perhaps the most popular and definitely the least strenuous is via a combination of the Appalachian Trail / Boulevard Trail / Alum Cave Trail. A hike combining these 3 will cover 13 tough miles, yet it is arguable that no other single peak in the entire southeast offers as many interesting and attractive features. This combination can be walked in one day, but would be far more enjoyable if undertaken over 2 or even 3 days. The summit alone could take an entire day to fully explore.

78

A Mt. LeConte visit involving this route would encompass the following distances:

- **Appalachian Trail** - Newfound Gap to Bouldevard Trail junction - 2.7 miles.
- **Boulevard Trail** - Appalachian Trail junction to Mt. LeConte summit and Alum Cave Trail junction - 5.3 miles.
- **Alum Cave Trail** - Boulevard Trail junction to Alum Cave Trail parking area on Newfound Gap Road - 4.9 miles.

Although it is certainly not the shortest route to Mt. LeConte's summit, the 8 mile hike along the Appalachian and Boulevard Trails involves the least amount of climbing. This section of the Appalachian Trail originates in Newfound Gap above 5,000 feet. The climb to LeConte's summit is a moderate 1,500 feet. There are too many outstanding features to highlight, though it should suffice to say it is most rewarding. Of special note are the groves of fraser fir and red spruce found along the route. One particularly outstanding section of these rare trees is along the initial 2 miles of the Boulevard Trail after it leaves the Appalachian Trail. This section conjures up images more appropriate to central Canada than eastern Tennessee.

Views along the trail are spectacular, and alternate from north to south. The grade does not exceed moderate levels until the last mile, when the final ascent up LeConte's northern face takes place.

Reward yourself when the trail finally gains the gently sloping summit ridge by visiting the two popular vantage points, Myrtle Point and Cliff Tops. Myrtle Point looks serenly to the east, and is best appreciated for its spectacular sunrises. The panorama atop Cliff Tops gazes south and west, and lies along the edge of the peak's sheer southern cliffs. Both locations offer views that are hard to top.

LeConte's long, narrow ridgeline is beautifully crowned with yet more fir and spruce. Additionally, two man-made structures are found atop the peak - Mt. LeConte shelter and LeConte Lodge. The 12-man LeConte shelter houses hikers lucky enough to secure a reservation for the primitive structure, while the rustic LeConte Lodge accomodates those visitors looking for a more civilized wilderness experience. For more details on LeConte Lodge, write LeConte Lodge, 250 Apple Valley Rd, Sevierville, TN 37862. Reservations should be made months in advance.

The shortest trail off the summit is the Alum Cave Trail. This 5.3 mile path screams off the mountain's steep southern face and features many outstanding natural wonders. Spectacular views continue along this trail. Of particular note is a several hundred yard long segment just below the Cliff Tops area of the summit. Here the trail has been carved along sheer cliffs, and cables have been installed to steady dizzy hikers along the narrow, dangerous path. Note: avoid the Alum Cave Trail during periods of extreme cold or snow. This upper portion of the trail can become extremely icy, and the cables are often buried beneath this ice! You won't want to test your luck under these conditions.

Almost 2.7 miles down from the summit, the trail passes beneath massive Alum Cave Bluff. This huge, overhanging rock face reaches almost 100 feet high. The dry area beneath the overhang makes a great rest spot, and is quite a departure from the normal trail scenery. Just 1.5 miles from the parking area, the path ends its torturous descent at Arch Rock. The trail descends through a natural opening in the rock and emerges at a footbridge over scenic Styx Branch. This final 1.5 miles closely follows the cascading stream, offering a calm contrast to the dramatic high ground of LeConte.

Directions: The Newfound Gap parking area is located along Hwy 441 (Newfound Gap Road) approximately 20 miles north-west of Cherokee, NC and 15 miles southeast of Gatlinburg, TN. The Alum Cave Trailhead is approximately 4 miles northwest of Newfound Gap along Hwy 441.

Alternate Hikes: Mt. LeConte can be reached via several interesting trails. The Bullhead, Rainbow Falls and Trillium Gap Trails all ascend from the west or north. Additionally, a good side-trip to the 13 mile LeConte hike is to continue along the Appalachian Trail past the Boulevard junction to Charlie's Bunion, just 1.7 miles away. Charlie's Bunion is a very popular destination that features a rocky knob overlooking an area exposed by a landslide in years past. The vantage point rests atop sheer cliffs, and features excellent views to the west. Detailed park maps can be obtained at either of the park's visitors centers.

Mt. LeConte

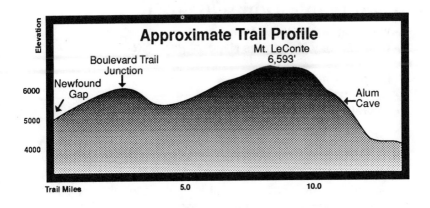

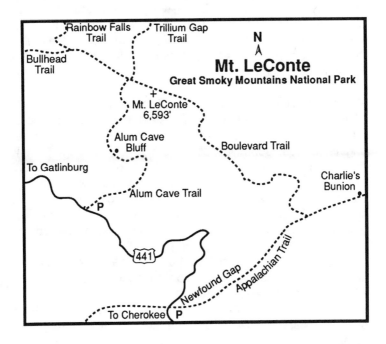

Clingman's Dome (6,642')

- via Clingman's Dome Trail
- Great Smoky Mountains National Park, NC

- **Length: 1 mile round trip**
- **Difficulty: moderate**
- **Overall elevation gain: approx. 400 feet**

Clingman's Dome is the highest peak in the Great Smoky Mountains National Park, rising 6,642 feet above sea level. This beautifully scenic yet convenient summit draws thousands of visitors during the warm summer months. The peak is easily conquered by even casual visitors via a steep, paved path that leads up to the summit. A circular observation tower crowns the mountain's high point, providing sweeping views of the park. Clingman's Dome is the perfect choice for those who like to get the view without getting the blisters. For those who enjoy the thrill of the challenge, numerous trails on the mountain provide several longer hiking options.

The Trail: The shortest route to Clingman's Dome is via the Clingman's Dome Trail. This short, steep trail winds 0.5 mile up the precipitous slopes of Forney Ridge to the summit. The trail originates in the southwest corner of the Forney Ridge parking area, and passes through the remnants of a once dense grove of fraser fir and red spruce. Just as with many of the other high Appalachian peaks, a great deal of Clingman's magnificent fir and spruce trees have been dying over the past decade. The mountain's upper southwest ridgeline is littered with dead and dying fir and spruce, both standing and fallen.

As with Mt. Mitchell and Grandfather Mountain to the northeast, speculation centers on air pollution and/or insect infestation. Either way, the results are tragic. The cool , shady walk to Clingman's summit of a decade ago is now through the bright sunshine, with only a moderate canopy of these once dominant conifers surviving.

Nevertheless, the trail is still very enjoyable. Interpretive plaques are spaced along the trail, pointing out various natural features and revealing a few of the forest's secrets. The interpretive markers also serve as rest areas, a point not lost on many visitors. Several benches have been strategically placed along the path, allowing visitors the opportunity to rest and enjoy the open forest views.

Just beyond 0.4 mile, the path begins to moderate, then turns east and levels out. The trail tunnels through a cool, fragrant grove of apparently healthy fir and spruce before culminating at the base of the dome's circular observation tower. This pedestaled tower rises well above the surrounding tree line, offering the best views in the entire park for the casual, hurried visitor. Photo markers line the outer tower wall, identifying various peaks and features visible from this outstanding vantage point. Perhaps the best views are to the northeast, where Mt. Collins rises in the foreground and massive Mt. LeConte dominates the horizon just seven miles distant. The tower is also accessible via the Appalachian Trail, which crosses the peak only 50 yards away. Clingman's Dome is notably the highest point along the 2,100 mile long pathway.

Clingman's Dome remains one of the most popular spots in the Smokies year round, though "unofficially" closed in the winter months. Officially, the 7.6 mile long Clingman's Dome Road (or Skyway) is closed due to excessive snow and ice above 6,000 feet. Nevertheless, hikers and bikers often venture out to the cold, windswept peak. Hikers may choose to walk the 7.7 mile Appalachian Trail segment or stroll along the 7.6 mile open road. Either choice offers magificent, scenic vistas. The road is a popular choice among mountain bikers, many of whom are attracted to the challenging snow and ice. One might be tempted to try biking the Skyway during the Spring or Summer months, but be forewarned - the 1,500 foot climb to Clingman's Dome and the heavy auto traffic may tempt you to reconsider.

Directions: The Skyway begins along Newfound Gap Road (Hwy 441) just yards south of Newfound Gap. Proceed along the Skyway 7.6 miles to the Forney Ridge parking area. The trail to Clingman's Dome begins in the southwest corner of the parking lot.

Additional Hikes: Numerous additional hikes are available on Clingman's Dome. Besides the famous Appalachian Trail segment that stretches 7.7 miles from Newfound Gap to the summit, the Forney Ridge Trail and the Forney Creek Trail are good choices for hiking. A 1.5 mile walk down the Forney Ridge Trail to scenic Andrews Bald is highly recommended. Visit either of the park's visitors centers for detailed maps.

From Clingman's Dome, massive Mt. LeConte rises to the northeast. Note the photo marker in the foreground.

Clingman's Dome

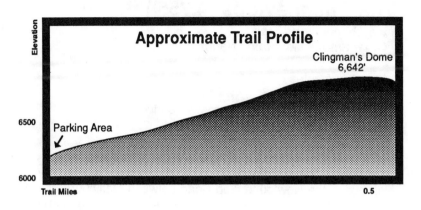

Approximate Trail Profile

Elevation

Clingman's Dome
6,642'

6500

Parking Area

6000

Trail Miles

0.5

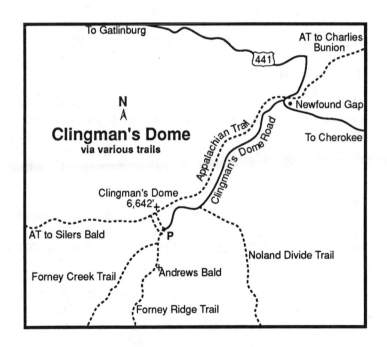

To Gatlinburg

AT to Charlies
Bunion

441

N

Newfound Gap

Clingman's Dome
via various trails

Appalachian Trail

Clingman's Dome Road

To Cherokee

Clingman's Dome
6,642'

AT to Silers Bald

P

Noland Divide Trail

Forney Creek Trail

Andrews Bald

Forney Ridge Trail

The Chimneytops (4,755')
• via Chimneytops Trail
• Great Smoky Mountains National Park, TN

• **Length: 4 miles round trip**
• **Difficulty: strenuous**
• **Overall elevation gain: approx. 1,400 feet**

Visitors to the Great Smoky Mountains National Park often notice 2 steep stone pillars jutting precariously into the sky high above the Newfound Gap Road between Gatlinburg and Newfound Gap. These 2 pillars are the Chimneytops, long recognized as one of the Smoky Mountain's trademarks. These rocky outcroppings soar almost 150 feet into the air, providing sensational park views. A relatively short but exhilarating hike combines with outstanding scenery to create one of the park's most popular trails. Though the 1,400 foot climb may intimidate some would-be visitors, the views from this Smokies version of "Twin Peaks" is well worth the effort.

The Trail: The 2 mile climb to the Chimneytops begins at an elevation of 3,400 feet, and quickly descends to a series of highly enjoyable footbridges that cross the rushing West Prong Little River and Road Prong just above their noisy junction. This photo-rich location is worth the visit even if you have no intention of climbing to the summit. This spot is usually quite crowded with camera toting visitors.

Once across Road Prong, the path turns sharply left and begins a moderate ascent along the scenic, cascading stream. At mile 0.7 another footbridge is reached. This bridge again spans Road Prong, then directs the path through a lushly forested area known as Beech Flats Cove. This area is rich in enormous hardwoods and is colorfully splashed with rich rhododendrons.

A trail junction is reached at mile 0.9. The Road Prong Trail forks to the left from this junction, climbing a laboring 2.4 miles up to the Appalachian Trail and Clingmans Dome Road just west of Newfound Gap.

A small wooden sign at this junction reminds you that 1.1 miles still lies between you and your destination, the Chimneytops. This next stretch of trail is bound to be your favorite, and

86

is primarily responsible for giving the trail its "strenuous" rating. The next 0.5 mile in particular is quite difficult, and includes a steep, straight ahead portion sure to wind even the most seasoned hiker. The fact that the path is somewhat eroded and quite rocky doesn't help either. The only real saving grace is that hikers are rewarded with a small, splashing brook that tumbles alongside the trail for part of this section. The brook is highlighted by a 20 foot waterfall that beckons hikers to stop and take a breather.

As the path nears the top of the ridge, it begins to snake along a series of broad, moderate switchbacks. The grade mercifully eases as the path circles around the steep ridgeline. At mile 1.7, the trail levels and even dips slightly as it rounds one last narrow bend. Beyond this curve, the unmistakeable profiles of the Chimneytops can be glimpsed through openings in the forest canopy. A steep, narrow finger of a ridge spans the distance over to the twin spires, requiring hikers to scramble through tangles of exposed roots beneath towering hemlocks. The trail seemingly ends at the base of the first spire, but the thousands of visitors over the years have worn numerous routes around the rocky outcroppings.

The Chimneytops are composed of an interesting shale-like rock that is quite rough to the touch. A feeling of vertigo is not uncommon as visitors gaze up the towering spires. Although they only rise about 150 feet above the ridge, the climb can be both tricky and dangerous. If a fear of heights is one of your problems, it is best to enjoy the view from the base of the rocks. For the courageous at heart, the scramble to the top provides truly breath-taking panoramas of the park's central section. To the east, the massive bulk of Mt. LeConte dominates the view. If you are familiar with the famous peak, you can pick out numerous details along this mountain. To your southeast, Mt. Mingus rises. To the west, Sugarland Mountain and the plateau region of Tennessee compete for your attention.

Besides looking something like chimneys from a distance, these outcroppings have something else in common with their namesakes. Namely, interesting openings in the tops of the spires. A natural hole burrows into the chimney and reaches almost 30 feet down. DO NOT ENTER these openings for any reason!

In the winter months, snow can make this trail and the Chimneytops extremely hazardous. Icy patches both along the path and on the chimneys are quite normal in the colder months.

and can ruin your hike in a hurry. The rock face can become quite slippery in wet weather, and it should go without saying that the Chimneytops are no place to be during thunderstorms! While the area can be dangerous in bad weather, when conditions are right this can be one of the most unusual and delightful summits in all the South.

Directions: The Chimneytops Trail begins along the Newfound Gap Road, 9.8 miles east of the Gatlinburg entrance to the Great Smoky Mountains National Park. A paved parking area lies along the south shoulder of the road, and the trail begins beyond the park service information board.

The Chimneytops

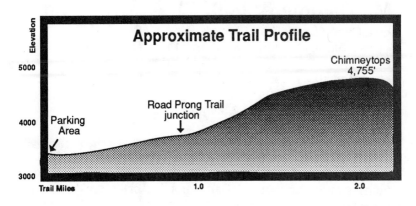

Approximate Trail Profile

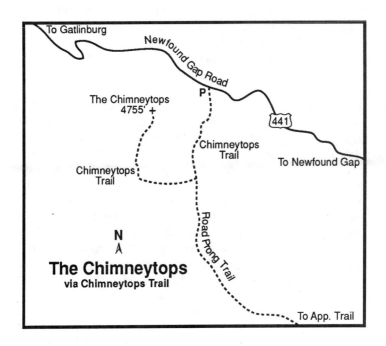

The Chimneytops
via Chimneytops Trail

Mt. Cammerer (4,928')
• via Cosby Creek Trail / Appalachian Trail
• Great Smoky Mountains National Park, TN

• **Length: 10.4 miles round trip**
• **Difficulty: strenuous**
• **Overall elevation gain: 2,500 feet**

An awe-inspiring 360 degree panoramic view of the northeastern portion of the Great Smokies range can be gained from the rocky summit of Mt. Cammerer, one of the park's lesser known major peaks. A challenging combination of trails climbs from Cosby Campground to the ridgeline summit, making for an outstanding day hike. Various connector trails lace this portion of the park, creating many outstanding variations in possible routes. This hike features cascading Cosby Creek, ever-changing forests, and stunning ridgeline views of the Cumberland Plateau region to the north. Mt. Cammerer was named in honor of Arno B. Cammerer, former park service director.

The Trail: This outstanding hike to Mt. Cammerer's summit begins in the southeastern corner of Cosby Campground. The initial 2.5 miles is along the Cosby Creek Trail, one of the park's shortest and steepest Appalachian connector trails. Initially, the path runs predominately flat through a forest of shady mature hardwoods. The first few hundred yards pass the campground water storage tank and old, concrete reservoirs. At mile 0.5, the trail crosses Cosby Creek via a single-lane log bridge, just downstream of a particularly scenic cascade. The next 0.5 mile winds alongside the splashing creek, tunnelling beneath massive, ancient helocks, past lush rhododendron groves, and beside thousands of deep, green moss-covered rocks. The grade remains mild to moderate. Enjoy it while it lasts.

From mile 1.0 to 2.5, the trail earns its "strenuous" ranking, gaining over 1,500 feet en route to Low Gap (which doesn't seem particularly well named on this hike) and the Appalachian Trail junction. Cosby Creek begins to diminish noticeably as numerous tributaries branch off and rise deep into the mountain coves. The path snakes alongside steep slopes, closely following the mountain's natural contours. The grade ranges from moderate to steep, but is always relentless. Frequent breaks make the climb quite a bit more tolerable. Views back to the north toward Cosby Campground are spectacular! The final few hundred yards to Low Gap moderate appreciably, and stopping to rest awhile at the gap is considered mandatory. The Appalachian Trail junction occurs in the heart of the large, open gap. To the west, the Appalachian Trail winds for 8.4 miles to Mt. Guyot. Straight ahead to the south, Walnut Bottoms is 2.3 miles distant. To the east, Mt. Cammerer looms, still 2.7 miles distant.

The Appalachian Trail rises moderately after leaving Low Gap toward Mt. Cammerer. The grade along this section is much more forgiving than along the Cosby Creek Trail, rising only about 700 feet along the next 2.1 miles. This portion of the ridgeline offers outstanding views of the flat plateau region to the north. It is fascinating to observe the way the mountainous region of the Appalachians disappears into the flatlands so quickly. Approximately 1 mile above Low Gap, near mile 3.5 of the hike, the relatively flat ridgeline containing Mt. Cammerer appears before you at a sharp bend in the trail. The mountain's steep western slopes lie smothered in light green mountain laurel groves, and stand in stark contrast to the surrounding forests.

The path attains the crest of the ridge and continues almost flat in spots to the junction with the Mt. Cammerer spur trail at mile 4.6. This spur trail branches off to the north, following a slightly undulating ridge out to the summit. This spur trail is a delight to follow, winding through dense heath-type groves of short, gnarled trees and undergrowth. Rock outcroppings abound along the high ridgeline, and several stretches of path are quite eroded and muddy from years of heavy hiker traffic.

The spur trail ends 0.6 mile from the Appalachian Trail, an exhausting 5.2 miles from Cosby Campground. Mt. Cammerer's summit is perched at the edge of an almost sheer ridge, and the summit features an old, weather-worn stone observation tower. The lower floor of the tower is accessible, but contains nothing other than memories. An adventurous visitor could scramble through one of the upper floor windows to gain access to the building, but the views are no better from the inside. The main drawing card here is the view, and it is certainly not disappointing. To the south, massive Mt. Sterling rises above you. To the west, you can gaze down onto Cosby Campground and Gabes Mountain. To the north, flatlands seem to stretch out into infinity. The

Snowbird Mountains rise to the east. One can gaze down to the north and easily follow I-40 and the Pigeon River along the base of the mountain. Enjoy your stay. Although there isn't much open ground to explore, numerous rocky slopes make great spots to lunch or to relax and enjoy the view. The 5.2 mile return hike to Cosby Campground is long and tiring, and the pronounced descent sure to be tough on the knees and ankles.

Directions: From Gatlinburg, take Hwy 73 east to Hwy 32 in Cosby, TN. Turn right onto Hwy 32 and follow for 1 mile to Cosby Road on your right. Proceed to the campground and park at the amphitheatre parking area. Walk up the main park road to the southeastern corner of the campground. The trail begins at a gated access road and is marked by a trail sign.

Alternate Hikes: One could just about fill a book describing all of the alternate hikes or routes through this area. Other trails that tie into the Appalachian Trail in this portion of the park include the Lower Mt. Cammerer Trail, Chestnut Branch Trail, Big Creek Trail, and Snake Den Ridge Trail. Visit one of the park visitors centers and obtain a detailed park map for more information.

Mt. Cammerer

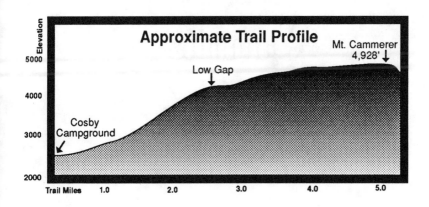

Approximate Trail Profile

Mt. Cammerer
4,928' ↓

Low Gap

Cosby
Campground

Elevation

5000

4000

3000

2000

Trail Miles   1.0   2.0   3.0   4.0   5.0

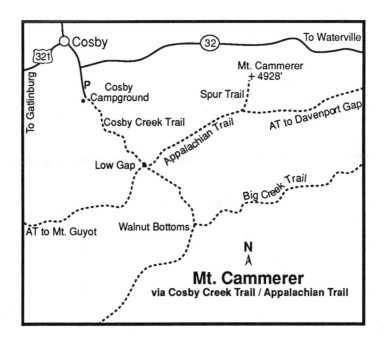

Cosby

To Waterville

32

321

To Gatlinburg

P   Cosby
Campground

Cosby Creek Trail

Mt. Cammerer
+ 4928'

Spur Trail

Appalachian Trail

AT to Davenport Gap

Low Gap

Big Creek Trail

AT to Mt. Guyot

Walnut Bottoms

N
⅄

Mt. Cammerer
via Cosby Creek Trail / Appalachian Trail

Summits
of the
South

Visitor's Guide to 25
Southern Appalachian Mountains

Appendix

Summits of the South

Summit	Elevation	Trail Length	Difficulty
1. Mt. Mitchell	6,684'	0.25	easy
2. Clingman's Dome	6,642'	1.0	moderate
3. Mt. LeConte	6,593'	10-16	strenuous
4. Tennent Mtn.	6,040	7.5	moderate
5. Grandfather Mtn.	5,954'	4.4	strenuous
6. Mt. Pisgah	5,721'	3.0	moderate
7. Standing Indian	5,499'	5.0	moderate
8. Yellow Mtn.	5,127'	9.6	strenuous
9. Cheoah Bald	5,062'	8.6	strenuous
10. Mt. Cammerer	5,025	10.4	strenuous
11. Whiteside Mtn.	4,930'	2.0*	moderate
12. Scaly Mtn.	4,804'	3.0	strenuous
13. Brasstown Bald	4,784'	1.2	moderate
14. Chimney Tops	4,755'	4.0	strenuous
15. Rabun Bald	4,696'	1.0	moderate
16. Chimneytop Mtn.	4,618'	3.0	strenuous
17. Blood Mtn.	4,458'	4.4	strenuous
18. Tray Mtn.	4,430'	1.8	moderate
19. Looking Gls Rck	3,969'	6.2	strenuous
20. Big Cedar Mtn.	3,737'	2.6	moderate
21. Wildcat Mtn.	3,730'	1.5	moderate
22. Black Rock Mtn.	3,640'	2.0*	moderate
23. Table Rock	3,157'	6.0	strenuous
24. Yonah Mtn.	3,156'	1.0	moderate
25. Fort Mtn.	2,854'	1.3*	easy

Trail Lengths shown generally denote the most direct or easiest route to the summit.

Trail Lengths with an * denote loop trails and provide the total distance. Other mileage given denotes round trip distance.

Lightning Safety

Few areas are as dangerous as the summit of a mountain during a thunderstorm or severe weather. Avoid any high, open area during threatening conditions **at all costs!** If you are caught outside during a thunderstorm, follow these general lightning safety rules:

- Do not stand beneath a structure that can act like a natural lighting rod, such as a tall, isolated tree or structure.
- Avoid standing higher than the surrounding landscape, such as on a **mountaintop**, hilltop, open field, beach or boat.
- Get out and away from the water.
- Avoid seeking shelter in small **isolated** sheds or buildings.
- Stay away from metal pipes, railings, fences or other metal structures that could draw lightning to you.
- Get off and away from tractors, motorcycles, golf carts, bikes. Do not hold golf clubs, tools, or other metal objects.
- In a forest, seek shelter in a low area in a grove of living trees. In open areas, seek a low place such as a ravine.
- If you are isolated in a level field or open area and feel your hair stand on end, immediately drop to your knees and bend forward, putting your hands on your knees. **Lightning is about to strike! Do not lie flat on the ground!**

First Aid for Lightning Victims:

    Quick, decisive action is required to save lightining victims.
- **Treat the apparent dead first**. Those unconcious but breathing may recover spontaneously.
- Mouth to mouth resuscitation should be administered to those not breathing within 4 to 6 minutes to avoid brain damage. Mouth-to-mouth resuscitation should be administered once every 5 seconds to adults and once every 3 seconds to infants and children.
- If victim is not breathing and has no pulse, administer cardio-pulminary resuscitation. This should be administered by those with proper training.
- Medical attention should also be given to victims who appear temporarily stunned or otherwise unhurt, since there may be hidden effects.

Travel Hints

• Enjoy the adventures of a forest experience, but do not take unnecessary chances. An illness which is normally minor can become serious in high elevations. If you get sick, try to get out of the mountains, or at least to a lower elevation while you can still travel.

• Know the locations of the Ranger Stations and hospitals near your route of travel. Leave an itenerary with friends. Take detailed maps and a whistle with you.

• If you think you are lost, stay calm and do not panic. Sit down and determine your location with your head, not your legs. Wandering under panic conditions usually will only make matters worse.

• In fog, storms or at night, stop and make camp in a sheltered place. Gather plenty of fuel and build a small warming fire in a safe place. Be sure to extinguish it completely before leaving.

• Three of anything (shouts, smoke, fires, whistles) are a sign of distress. If seen or heard, help will soon be on the way.

• It is wise not to travel alone, but if you must, stay on frequently used trails in case of sickness or injury.

• Carry a lightweight groundcloth or plastic which can be used for shelter should it rain.

• Bring sunburn lotion, insect repellent and lip balm. It is advisable to carry dark glasses.

• Be alert for poisonous plants and animals. Poison oak grows to altitudes of about 5,000 feet. Rattlesnakes can be found as high as 9,000 feet.

• Sudden mountain storms are common, especially in afternoon and evening. Observe all lightning safety guidelines in severe weather. (See lightning safety rules - page 96).

• Sign all trail registers. The register will help others find you if you become lost. These trail registers are also used to determine which trails receive the most use and should have priority for trail maintenance.

Equipment

- Maps (detailed topographical if possible)
- Water (be sure to purify if taken from stream or spring)
- Compass
- Waterproof Matches
- Flashlight
- Rainsuit or poncho
- Whistle
- First Aid Kit
- Moleskin or Duct Tape for blisters
- Hiking Stick

Clothing

- Choose clothing to fit the particular season and trail conditions you will face. Popular, heavily travelled pathways are normally wide and relatively free of briars, limbs and undergrowth. These type paths are fine for lightweight clothing or shorts in warmer weather. Wilderness or primitive trails may require thicker, more protective clothing. Colder conditions must be anticipated and planned for. Layering is the preferred method for dealing with changing cold weather conditons. This allows the hiker the chance to put-on or take-off as much as is needed to remain comfortable. Be prepared for any conditions!

Blisters

- Blisters are an all-too-common problem among hikers, especially when hiking along steep grades such as in the Southern Appalachians. Be sure to wear proper footwear, including correct socks. Two pairs of socks are recommended for hiking - a lightweight inner pair and heavy (preferably wool) outer pair. Shoes should be well broken in before attempting any long hikes. The alternative is a miserable and quite unforgettable wilderness experience !

Pace

• One of the most important considerations on a summit hike is that of **proper pacing**. Novice hikers often greatly overestimate the amount of terrain they are able to cover, and underestimate the difficulty of mountain trails. While 3 mile per hour is not unusual on level terrain, most experienced hikers find that **1 to 2 miles per hour** is more realistic and enjoyable on trails requiring strenuous climbs.

Do not forget that you are in the wilds to enjoy nature and the beautiful scenery. **Plan ample time into your schedule to rest, relax and wander around these magnificent summits.**

Drinking Water

• **Purify all drinking water** obtained in the wild! Even though most spring water or stream water obtained high in the Appalachians is usually pure, man-made contaminants or natural bacteria can still be found in it.

Purification tablets are available at most outdoor shops. **Chlorine bleach** can also be used. Add 2 drops of chlorine bleach per quart of water. Follow directions on the package for purification tablets. If these are not available, **boiling the water** is acceptable, and probably the best overall purification method. **Water purification filters** are also becoming increasingly popular.

In emergency situations, it may be impossible to purify your drinking water. If possible, **drink only fast flowing water from high, small streams. Try to avoid drinking standing water or water around heavily used trails or campsites, particularly downstream of a trail crossing or campsite.**

Hypothermia

Hypothermia is a very serious condition where the body temperature lowers due to exposure to cold. **Hypothermia can be fatal** if not quickly diagnosed and treated. Surprisingly, hypothermia can occur in air temperatures as high as 41 degrees F. Wearing cold, wet clothing is one of the most common ways of contracting hypothermia, although prolonged exposure to cold, even in dry clothing, can place you at risk.

One of the first danger signals of hypothermia is **shivering**. If this occurs, treat it immediately. **Prolonged shivering** means that the condition is worsening. If the individual displays a **loss of coordination, slurred speech, poor judgement or weakness**, the situation has become very serious. Usually, the final symptom of hypothermia is **unconciousness**.

There are a number of things that can be done for someone suffering from hypothermia. **First, get the victim into warm, dry cothing. Force the person to rest and give them hot food and hot drinks. If the condition is advanced, put the individual into a sleeping bag with another person. Build a fire and put up a shelter for the victim, if possible. When the person is able, get them to a hospital as soon as possible. Never continue a trip when someone has suffered from hypothermia.**

Above all, please consider this condition as **very serious**. Hypothermia can be a killer for those not familiar with its symptoms.

A Word About the Weather

As a general rule, **expect the unexpected** when hiking the Southern Appalachian peaks. Climate conditions vary greatly with altitude. Higher elevations generally remain much cooler and wetter than areas of lower elevations in the same vicinity. Temperaures may lose as much as 5 degrees F per each 1000 foot increase in altitude. That warm, sunny 70 degree day in the valley could possibly be in the 40's or 50's atop one of the higher peaks.

Many of the higher summits, such as Grandfather Mountain, Mt. Mitchell or Clingman's Dome, greatly influence their own weather. Various mountain profiles have a funnelling effect on wind currents, greatly increasing wind speed and precipitation. It is not uncommon to experience winds exceeding hurricane force during storms atop these summits. Again, **be prepared for any conditions in any season**. Just ask any Appalachian Trail hiker who has experienced one of the Smokies infamous April snowstorms.

In the wintertime, snow is very common on the higher peaks, often not melting completely until April. Points such as Newfound Gap in the Great Smoky Mountains National Park receive an annual average of 70+ inches of snow per year! Ice patches can form across the trails, creating very hazardous conditions. Winter hikers, especially on those trails exceeding 5,000 feet, should **take all precautions against the cold.**

On the opposite extreme, summer temperatures are usually comfortably cool, yet can become quite cold at night on the mountaintops. Heavy rainfall occurs year round, though the heaviest amounts usually take place during the winter, spring and summer. Rainfall amounts exceeding 80 inches per year classify many of the higher peaks as temperate rainforests. Raingear is essential!

Expect the unexpected!

NOTES

NOTES

NOTES